Reflections

To Samina
and family

Richard Pawson

Richard.
6/10/23

Woodlark Press
Henley-on-Thames

978-1530544554

First edition

Cover photograph taken by the author in Bangladesh, 1984.

Set in Baskerville Old Face.

Published by:

Woodlark Press
Chiltern House
45 Station Road
Henley on Thames
RG9 1AT

Richard Pawson has enjoyed a career that has spanned software development, journalism, product marketing, robotic engineering, and toy design. It started in January 1977 when he joined Commodore for a gap year before university, and three weeks later the company announced the world's first personal computer. He has a BSc in Engineering Science, a PhD in Computer Science, and is a part-qualified patent and trademark attorney. He has written two previous books: *The Robot Book* (Windward, 1985) and *Naked Objects* (J Wiley, 2002, co-authored with Robert Matthews). He lives in Henley-on-Thames where he rows occasionally, and not very well.

Moon Landing 1

Drawing on the Right Side of the Brain 5

O, Jerusalem 9

Altitude 13

Highways 17

The Right Stuff 21

With worn-out tools 25

Forty shades of Green 29

Unfolding the design 33

Faster than the sun 39

Solution 43

Peace like a river 49

The day the universe changed 55

Music of the Spheres 59

Prometheus Unbound 63

Reserve 69

Mastery 73

Minimum 77

High Rise 81

Standing on the shoulders of giants 85

Field of Dreams 89

Hospitality 91

Underworld 97

Tradition 101

Thanksgiving 107

Index 113

Acknowledgements

This book is a series of reflections on personal encounters – with people, with places, and with ideas – that have taken place over the last forty years.

I would like to express my gratitude to the individuals who, knowingly or unknowingly, feature in the book, several of whom have had a significant impact on my thinking, my beliefs, or my career.

I have always enjoyed stories, both hearing them and telling them, and I like to think that I have a good memory for the details of a story. But that memory is not infallible, and if I have misrepresented any events, and in particular the words or actions of any of the individuals mentioned, then I certainly apologise.

I would like to thank my wife, Ann, and children, Guy and Aruna, for proof-reading the drafts and providing constructive feedback. Responsibility for any remaining errors, however, is mine alone.

Richard Pawson, Henley-on-Thames, 2016

Moon Landing

J ust a couple of hundred feet above the surface I increased the fuel burn rate to the maximum, slowing the rate of descent. Seconds later the lunar module touched down on the moon. The astronaut next to me offered his congratulations.

I wasn't really on the moon, obviously; and I wasn't at the controls of a real lunar module; I was at home playing a game of Lunar Lander on my personal computer. But the man standing next to me was a real astronaut, and he *had* successfully landed on the moon. His name was James (Jim) Irwin, and he was the Lunar Module Pilot for Apollo 15.

That he was taking a keen interest in my activity was less due to the nature of the game and more to the fact that he had never seen a personal computer before. Nor had most people – this was 1978. It was a Commodore PET 2001/8, the first production personal computer in the world. I'd got my hands on one of the first batch to be shipped to the UK, and brought it home – to my parents' home, that is, since I was still at university. Jim wasn't there to see me, or my computer: he was there to meet my father and was speaking at his church, but I couldn't pass up the opportunity to engage him.

By the standards of today's computer games, Lunar Lander was very simple. You controlled the fuel burn rate by hitting the numeric keys, 0 through 9, and a real-time display showed the altitude, vertical velocity, elapsed time, and remaining fuel. The lunar module was rendered in simple graphics, as was the surface of the moon below; if you hit the ground at more than the permitted maximum impact velocity – which happened all too often, usually because you had run out of fuel – crude animation showed the lunar module breaking apart on impact.

'Of course, this must seem simplistic compared to the real thing', I offered. 'No,' said the man who'd done it for real, 'that's about what it was like'. I assumed that he was just being polite, humouring this enthusiastic young man. He asked me a lot of questions about the Commodore PET and what else it was capable of doing.

Seven years later, on my first stay in Boston, Massachusetts, I visited the Computing Museum. One of the many interactive exhibits was a complete life-size simulation of the real landing computer from an Apollo Lunar Module. With a shock I realised that Jim had been telling the truth: the real device had been little more sophisticated than the Lunar Lander game, and likely had no more computing power than my early home computer. It was a stark illustration of just how much the Apollo missions depended upon the mental faculties and manual flying skills of the astronauts. On the first landing, Commander Neil Armstrong had to avoid an unexpected crater on the chosen landing site, and finally settled the craft with just 25 seconds-worth of fuel remaining. And lunar module pilot Buzz Aldrin was chosen, in part, for his extraordinary skills in calculating three-dimensional docking manoeuvres in his head.

It's not just technology that has changed dramatically, but social attitudes also. We don't face quite the same threat of nuclear Armageddon now as in the height of the cold war; but nor are we as optimistic about building a better future.

And smaller things too. Jim Irwin was the first of the Apollo astronauts to die, in 1991. When I read his obituary in the newspaper, I asked my mother if she remembered his visit. 'Very clearly,' she said, her expression rather hard to read. Jim had come with his wife and five children. My mother had cooked lamb chops; on seeing them one of the family had announced that they were vegetarian, causing my mother a certain amount of embarrassment, having nothing else prepared. My mother was used to catering for my father's many visitors, but in 1978 a vegetarian visitor was perhaps as unusual as one of the twelve men who'd walked on the moon.

II

Drawing on the Right Side of the Brain

'I gave you 20 minutes to perform the task, yet every one of you was back in the room in under 15 minutes.' She was right - we all felt that we'd done as much as we could and there was no point just sitting there staring into space. 'Well we're going to repeat that task at the end of the week, and two things will astonish you. The first is the difference in the quality of what you have produced,' - this was hard for us to believe - 'and the second is that every one of you will complain you didn't have enough time, even though, on Friday, I'm going to give you *four hours*'. The woman was clearly delusional - if we'd finished in less than twenty minutes the first time, what could we possibly be doing for four hours? As it turned out, she was right on both counts.

The task was to draw a self-portrait; the woman was Dr Betty Edwards, author of *Drawing on the Right Side of the Brain*, one of the most remarkable women I have met, and a lovely person with it. The premise of her book is that most adults can't draw any better than when they were 8 years old. Why should this be, when, for most people, every other skill – physical, intellectual, social – continues to develop for many years? Betty claims to be able to right this deficiency, and teach any adult to draw. Her ideas were inspired, in part, by the work of the neuroscientist Roger Sperry, who was the first to identify that different thinking skills are concentrated in different physical locations within the brain's cortex. In particular, he determined that symbolic processing (such as language and logic) is *for many people* concentrated in the left-hemisphere, where spatial processing is commonly concentrated in the right.

Now it needs to be said that there is a lot of tosh talked about left-brained vs. right-brained thinking or, worse, left-brained vs. right-brained people. In recent years, even Betty herself has been more cautious about the localisation of the functions, but her core idea remains valid - that an inability to draw is due to the relative dominance of symbolic processing over spatial processing as a person grows. And her techniques for overcoming that dominance are highly effective.

I bought the book in 1989 in a bookstore in Santa Cruz, California, on the recommendation of a member of the bookstore's staff. That's one of the reasons I love bookstores in America: the staff will talk to you about the books just for the pleasure of it. English bookstores have been very slow on the uptake, and I have little sympathy when they bleat about not being able to compete with the Internet, as they typically don't offer any better service than the online retailers.

That Christmas break, I spent three days working my way through her exercises, designed to show you the difference between the two styles of thinking, and at the end of three days was able to draw a pleasingly-recognisable pencil portrait of Winston Churchill, copied from a photograph. (The drawing of Churchill overleaf is not that first drawing, but another one that I made some years later, in chalk and charcoal).

Eight years later, I was introduced to Betty and we had the opportunity to collaborate on a brief project. I was designing a training course for IT managers to teach a different approach to problem-solving in software design known as 'object-orientation'. The course would be run, privately, at the Disney Institute in Florida. Each morning would start with Betty teaching them how to draw – the point being that the key to learning how to draw is to learn how to draw what you are actually seeing, not what your symbolic brain tells you it thinks it is looking at. Then Alan Kay, one of the pioneers of object-oriented design, and I would try to teach them object-oriented thinking, which also required them to learn to see the world in a different way. In the evenings, we went to the Disney kitchens to learn different cooking techniques.

I loved spending the time with Betty, and at the end of the course she invited me to attend, as her guest, one of her week-long full-time courses later that year. I have to say that it was one of the most rewarding weeks of my life. On the Friday afternoon of that course we were duly given four hours to draw a second self-portrait, and, as predicted, when the gong went we complained we weren't quite finished. Betty made us all pin up our artwork on the walls, the 20-minute Monday-morning version next to the 4-hour Friday-afternoon version. We drank some wine and admired each other's progress – many would not have believed on Monday morning that they'd have been willing to pin anything they'd drawn on a wall for others to appraise. It was quite emotional, but the emotions were not of embarrassment, as might have been predicted at the start, but of joy, and even of release.

7

III

O, Jerusalem

The narrow pathway of beaten earth was baked hard by the sun, but my eye was caught by the tiniest edge of something metallic embedded within it. I had to use my penknife to extract it: an expended rifle shell, .303 calibre, the type I had shot regularly on the rifle ranges at school. Brushing away the dirt, I could just make out the year of manufacture stamped on the rim - 1947. The war in Europe and the Far East had been long over by then, but I wasn't in Europe or the Far East; I was standing between the two, atop the wall of the old city of Jerusalem, near the Zion gate, scene of some of the fiercest fighting in the Israeli War of Independence in 1948.

One of the many things I love about the Middle-East in general, and Israel in particular, is the sense that compressed in every square metre of soil are centuries, often millennia, of history. The wall I was standing on was built by Suleiman the Magnificent in the sixteenth century, replacing (and relocating) the Roman walls, which in turn superseded earlier walls. And now I was holding in my hand a historical artefact from a 20th century conflict.

Beit She'an, in the north of Israel, is dominated by the well-preserved Roman theatre and cardo (market place), but in the course of an hour's stroll around the grounds you can see remains from the Egyptian, Hellenistic, Byzantine, Arab caliphate, Crusader, Mamluk, and Ottoman eras, spanning four millennia in total. Forty kilometres west of Beit She'an a mound stands proud of the plain. When archaeologists identified it as the ancient city of Megiddo (from which we get the name Armageddon), they faced the dilemma of when to stop digging. Should they risk destroying one well-preserved habitation in order to search for the possibility of an older one underneath it? In the end they decided to take one slice from the cake, digging down a narrow sector to ground level. In the process they discovered eight separate levels of civilisation each built on the ruins of the previous one.

While some of these sites are formally managed – you pay the entrance fee and take the guided tour – some of the most interesting sites are unmarked, left for each traveller to discover for themselves. On my most recent visit to Jerusalem I took a short walk before dinner, up the hill to the west of the old city. I wanted to see the restored windmill originally built in 1857 by Sir Moses Montefiore (great uncle to the contemporary historian and television presenter, Simon Sebag Montefiore). From the windmill I walked on up into a small suburban park, located just below the imposing King David Hotel. The park was empty but for the occasional dog walker. It was a lovely evening, and with the setting sun the golden stone of Jerusalem was turning to salmon pink.

In the middle of the park there is what looks like a small stone quarry, half-heartedly roped off, with discarded cans and puddles of stagnant water at the bottom. As I walked past it my eye was caught by something in the corner - a few steps leading down to a low doorway in the rock face. Scrambling down, I was able to confirm what I thought I had seen: in front of the doorway, to one side, and partly concealed in a deep stone trench, was a perfectly-cut disc of stone, approximately 120cm in diameter and 40cm thick. It was clearly intended to be rolled across the doorway, entry to which was now barred by a rusty, but solid, metal door. The scene was exactly like an illustration of the tomb in which, according to the Gospels, Christ was buried. Whatever one believes about what exactly took place in Jerusalem two thousand years ago, seeing a real version of that illustration is striking – all the more so because you won't find anything like it at the 'official' site of Christ's tomb, the Church of the Holy Sepulchre, nor at the alternative one, The Garden Tomb. (The latter has a rather more authentic-looking rock-hewn tomb, and the groove in front is claimed to be for a rolling stone, though the fact that the groove isn't level casts some doubt on the claim.)

Back at our hotel, a few minutes' research on the internet revealed that the site I had been looking at is well-known to archaeologists, even though it is unmarked on the ground. It is unquestionably a tomb from the first century AD, one of only a handful of examples in the region that feature a rolling-stone door. Inside the now-sealed doorway, apparently, are large rooms hewn from the rock and containing a couple of stone sarcophagi, but no skeletons, treasures or identifying marks; the tomb was either raided long ago for its valuables, or perhaps never actually used. For many years, archaeologists proposed that the tomb had been prepared by Herod the Great, for his family, but even that theory has lost ground since the discovery of a more likely site north of the city.

And why is this unmarked and virtually empty tomb now sealed off with a heavy steel door? The answer is that, yet again, it has played other roles across the centuries.

If you had been on this site on the morning of Monday 22nd July, 1946, you would have witnessed an unusual tableau: milkmen carrying heavy milk churns out of the tomb and up to the King David Hotel, where the churns were deposited in the basement as usual, next to one of the pillars. Shortly afterwards, the churns blew up – they were packed with 350 kilograms of explosives – bringing down a whole wing of the hotel that was used by the British military administration, killing 91 and injuring many others. That attack was planned and executed by the Irgun, a terrorist Zionist organisation committed to driving out the British administration. The leader of the Irgun at that time was Menachem Begin, who would later, as Israeli prime minister, sign the Camp David Accords, leading to the 1979 peace treaty with Egypt's Anwar Sadat.

Once again, a strong reminder not only of the centuries of history compressed into each square metre, but of the enduring conflicts in the region. I think it was Isaiah Berlin who first said it, though the quotation has been attributed to many others since: 'too much history and too little geography'.

IV

Altitude

'**P**lease take off your watches and give them to me. I'll place them here in the safe until we get back.' That wouldn't be for 10 days. Some of our group were hesitant - not about entrusting him with their valuables, but to be parted from something they depended upon. This was in 1984; the contemporary equivalent would be to ask people to part with their mobile phones for 10 days. 'You won't be needing them,' he went on, 'You'll be rising and going to bed with the sun. And, quite frankly, I don't want to be pestered with "what time's lunch?" or "when do we stop for the day?" You walk until you see where the Sherpas have stopped to cook your meal, or set up camp.'

We were in Kathmandu, about to travel by bus to Pokhara, where our trek would begin. There were about fifteen of us in the group, from all parts of the globe, mostly strangers to each other until the previous evening; but after ten days of trekking and camping in the rough, we would become quite intimately acquainted. Sitting around a camp fire every evening we'd discuss music and books, history and politics, aching muscles and bowel movements - or lack of them. The latter is a continual background concern when trekking; one of the more popular trails around the foothills of the Annapurnas was known as the 'Andrex trail', because every time you

13

popped into the bushes you could expect to find evidence of previous trekkers. The route we were taking, up to the foot of Machpuchare, wasn't so well-trodden, fortunately.

We had to carry everything we needed for ten days - tents, sleeping bags, food, cookware, fuel for the stoves, and clothes. The weight was not evenly distributed though. The trekkers carried a light day pack each. Everything else was carried by the Sherpas - slightly-built young men carrying loads up the mountain all day that many of us would have struggled to carry a few yards, the sinews in their legs as taut as bow-strings. The Sherpas were overseen by their Sirdar, named Ram, who allocated the load to each man in the mornings. From time to time we all worried about the ethics of the situation: were we exploiting them, or were we providing them with much-needed paid work?

Despite the loads, they would climb much faster than we, and by the time we got to the designated camp, they would have put up the heavy canvas tents, and the cook would have a meal under way. The diet was limited, but we were always just glad to have food and have it cooked for us - though it would be many years later before I could again face eating cauliflower soup or *dal bhat* (steamed rice with lentil soup).

Every morning we would wake to the 'dawn chorus' – the sound of the Sherpas bringing up the unpleasant contents of their lungs, tuberculosis being rife in Nepal. But generally they seemed happy and well, if poorly clad for the climate - many climbed without shoes. They would bring us hot tea, which would taste strongly of kerosene from the stove, and a small bowl of hot water for our ablutions.

For the first couple of days our trek took us through several small hamlets in the foothills. I noticed an

14

interesting pattern of economics: with each gain of a thousand feet the price of tea, locally harvested, dropped by half a Rupee, but the price of Coca-Cola, the other universal commodity, rose by one Rupee. Once above habitation we were reliant on what the Sherpas carried.

I think the highest we got was about 15,000 feet – no higher than the tallest mountain in Europe, and still 3000 feet lower than Everest base camp. The views were dramatic, but we all slept badly from a combination of the cold and the thinner air. The next day we descended several thousand feet, and the air tasted like wine.

We returned to Kathmandu where we enjoyed several more days relaxing and exploring before going our separate ways. I went on to Bangladesh, where I took the cover photograph for this book. But I deliberately left my watch in the safe in Kathmandu, and I have never worn one since.

V

Highways

The seven-seat Westwind III executive jet climbed steeply away from the runway at Hannover airport in Germany, and I felt myself being pushed deeper into the luxurious brown leather seat, and taking care not to spill my gin and tonic. I was sitting opposite Jack Tramiel, the chief executive of Commodore, who was staring pensively out of the generous-sized window next to him. 'You see that Autobahn we're crossing over?' he said, 'I built that.' I was puzzled; I knew the company he'd founded had started in typewriters before moving onto adding machines, then electronic calculators, and now personal computers; but he'd surely never been in the construction business? Then the penny dropped - he hadn't built that Autobahn as a businessman, he'd built it as a slave.

Jack was born into a Jewish family in Poland. In 1939 they were rounded up with other Jews and moved into a ghetto in Lodz, then subsequently to concentration camps. His mother was sent to Auschwitz and died there; he and his father were sent to a work camp near Hannover, where his father also died - Jack believed as victim of one of Joseph Mengele's inhuman experiments. Jack survived the work camps, to be rescued in 1945 by

17

American soldiers, by then in a desperate state of health. When his health recovered he emigrated to America and enlisted in the army, at least in part out of a sense of gratitude for his rescue, where he was assigned to a maintenance role. Upon leaving the army he set up a one-man typewriter repair business, soon moving onto selling manual- and electric-typewriters, then adding machines. In the late 1960s he saw the potential of the new electronic calculating machines, though they were initially expensive and clunky by modern standards. Eventually he built his company, Commodore, into one of the largest and most admired consumer electronics companies in the world, vertically integrated from silicon chip design and fabrication, to the production and marketing of calcula-tors, digital watches, and, eventually, the products for which the company became famous: personal computers.

Jack had a fearsome reputation: many of his senior staff dreaded the next 'Jack-attack', when he would fly in and tear their local operation apart, demanding higher performance and more economy. His attitude to his suppliers was legendary, far removed from the modern idea of a strategic partnership; as far as Jack was con-cerned, any dollar of profit being made by one of his suppliers was a dollar being stolen from him. Yet when one knew some of his life story, his pugnacious approach was a little easier to understand, if no easier to endure.

He told me that one time he needed to source industrial gold for use in silicon chip manufacture (gold was then used for the fine wires connecting the tiny chip to the surrounding package), and one supplier was offering a particularly low price. When Jack asked why the cost was so much lower than their competitors, the supplier explained that it was 'recycled' gold – a euphemism, it transpired, for 'extracted from the teeth of corpses'.

Understandably, given his experiences in the concentration camps, Jack threw the supplier out unceremoniously.

The irony of sitting in his personal jet and flying over the very roads he'd been forced to build as a Jewish prisoner was not lost on him, nor me.

I flew in a private jet only one other time, a year later; it was also a Westwind III, and also owned by Commodore, but in this one the leather seats were blue. I'd heard that the one I'd flown in previously had subsequently had to make an emergency landing after an electrical fire broke out at 30,000 feet, filling the cabin with smoke and resulting in a loss of main electrical power. Apparently, the fire had started when someone plugged in the coffee percolator a little too hard, and caused a short in the wiring harness behind. Jack Tramiel, his wife, and a number of senior Commodore executives were on board; fortunately the plane was able to make an emergency landing and they all survived.

It didn't seem to have put Jack off from buying another jet of the same model, though - or so I had assumed. Only once we were airborne did I learn that this was in fact the same jet, but with a complete internal re-fit. I declined the offer of a cup of coffee.

VI

The Right Stuff

I'd like to claim that I recognised him just from the finely chiselled features of his face, but in truth it was his clothes - who else wears two-tone shoes, a crisp white suit, and a Homburg to match? Besides, I was standing behind him.

We were waiting for the pedestrian lights to change - there was hardly any traffic, but thereabouts it was considered impolite to cross early. Standing in front of us were half-a-dozen college girls and the older gentleman. A truck came around the corner, rather close, and everyone involuntarily stepped backwards; the man stepped on my toe and turned to apologise - and that confirmed it. When he'd turned back I whispered to my colleague, 'That's Tom Wolfe' (pictured). In a swanky restaurant in New York's Upper East Side, surrounded by the city's literati, this would hardly be surprising. But we were in the small town of Chapel Hill, North Carolina. The town is home to the University of North Carolina, but the almost soporific atmosphere of its central crossroads seemed far removed from metropolitan urbanity.

The lights changed and we crossed the road. A few yards further on, the party in front - it transpired that they were all together – turned into a restaurant, the same one

21

we had booked. The man approached the maître d' saying, 'We have a reservation for a table of seven. The name is Wolfe'; if she recognised him she hid it well, though I rather doubt that she did.

We were, of course, too polite to eavesdrop on their conversation; the fact that we were seated three tables away had nothing to do with it. But we did speculate for a few minutes on what was taking place. My colleague suggested that Tom Wolfe might have been a guest speaker at a university event, and was now being taken out to dinner by the event committee, or other hand-picked student representatives. No, that didn't work - the table reservation wouldn't have been in his name. Perhaps one of the girls was his niece and he'd offered to take her and close friends to dinner to celebrate some recent achievement. Six seemed quite extravagant, though, and why all girls? Unable to come up with a convincing story, we talked for a while about his work instead.

I am a big fan: I think I've read all of Tom Wolfe's books. The novels, starting with *Bonfire of the Vanities*, are all superb, but I prefer the non-fiction. *The Right Stuff*, which sought to get under the skin of pioneering test pilots like Chuck Yeager, and the 'Mercury 7', the first seven putative astronauts selected for training by NASA, became the defining phrase for bravery and coolness under pressure. He didn't invent the idea of writing a piece of journalism with the pace and style of a novel, but he is the undisputed master of the technique, and it is fitting that the best anthology of such writing, *The New Journalism*, was compiled by him.

Two years after that dinner, his latest novel appeared: *I am Charlotte Simmons*. It is set in the prestigious DuPont University, a fictional amalgam of Duke, Princeton, and perhaps other east- coast campus colleges. In the front of the book, he acknowledges the contributions to his research (something he is famed for) from many people, mentioning *inter alia* students and faculty at Chapel Hill. So that, presumably, was what the dinner was for: research. Given that one of the recurring themes of the book is the sexual mores of college students, which won him the un-coveted Bad Sex Award from the London-based Literary Review, I'm rather relieved that we couldn't overhear the conversation.

VII

With worn-out tools

Isaac showed me to my bedroom and bathroom, and I was relieved to see a conventional bathtub, washbasin, and toilet; I hadn't known what to expect. But no water came out of the taps. The bedroom had mains electrical sockets on the walls. But no electricity came out of them. There was nothing unusual about Isaac's house - the neighbouring houses would have all been the same. Isaac could remember running water and mains electricity, but none of his children, the eldest in her mid-teens, had seen either. They drew every gallon that they needed from a well in the yard, and electricity came from a private generator, for just a few hours of the day. And all this was not in some out-of-the-way village: we were in the heart of a capital city - Monrovia, Liberia - which had been ravaged by years of civil war.

Isaac is a remarkable man, showing tremendous personal faith in the face of adversity, deprivation, and constant threat to life and limb. That threat came from drug-crazed militia, many of them young boys, armed with machetes and machine guns, and keen to use both to demonstrate their power. By the time of my visit to Liberia in 2008 the fighting had thankfully ended, and the country was politically stable again. But the scars – physical, emotional, economic – would take years to heal.

In the midst of that strife, Isaac had decided to set up a training institute, to help provide the kind of skills that Liberia would eventually need when, or if, the civil war ended – such as computing and secretarial skills. They started with a single, outdated, desktop personal computer, running on a tiny generator. Our church (the pastor had known Isaac for many years, having lived in Liberia himself) then started to collect old computers and other goods and send them out in containers to Isaac, along with some financial gifts. The success of the institute, however, owes far more to the extraordinary efforts of Isaac and his local team than to any external help. By the time of my visit they had scores of students attending the institute part-time, using dozens of re-cycled computers powered by a large diesel generator in the yard outside, and all sharing a single low-bandwidth satellite link to the Internet.

On my first day I was given a tour of the facilities. The secretarial students in particular impressed me - young ladies, looking professional in their navy blue uniforms with brightly patterned neck-scarves. In some respects it felt like moving back a few decades, but I mean that in a positive way: as I entered the room the teacher was explaining all the correct uses of a semi-colon. How many students in Britain, I wonder, could articulate even one of them? Later on I was invited to interview some of the students, all of whom seemed keen to talk. I found it humbling as one after another told me of their personal family circumstances, and how they had scraped together the fees – which are kept to an absolute minimum – to take the courses.

When I asked them what they hoped to gain from it, the answer was always the same: to get a job with an NGO (Non-Governmental Organisation). This left me with mixed feelings. Post-war Liberia was awash with NGOs assisting in its rehabilitation. As we drove in from the airport, passing several military checkpoints, every other car that we passed seemed to be a white 4x4 with 'UN' in large black letters on the side; at the airport there had been similarly-marked planes parked on the apron. Clearly NGOs bring money into the country, both as explicit aid, and in the form of employment and services; but they also distort the economy.

In the course of my stay, Isaac took me to three different places to buy food. The first was the local market: vibrant, noisy, smelling of spices and caged small livestock – much as you would see throughout Africa. Later we went to a down-town grocery store, where the better-off locals could buy tinned and packaged goods. There was no self-service: a counter running around three sides of the shop separated customers from the goods on the shelves behind. Then finally, he took me to another store down the street. Inside it was icy-cold from the air-conditioning, brightly-lit, packed with blemish-free fresh produce and convenience meals; we might have been in a home counties Waitrose, with prices to match. There weren't many locals to be seen shopping here - this was the preserve of the diplomats, military, and NGOs.

We also visited a number of other training institutes set up more recently by NGOs. Where Isaac had an eclectic range of re-cycled and re-conditioned PCs, some of these other facilities had shiny new equipment with large flat screens. I felt a twinge of jealousy on Isaac's behalf; if he felt it he kept it well masked. But I saw something much deeper in his organically-grown and locally-managed operation - both more sustainable and more sustaining.

I am not sure what I had really hoped to accomplish from my visit. I gave a couple of technical lectures to some of the more advanced computing students, and helped Isaac gain some publicity on national radio, but increasingly I just felt helpless and humbled by what I observed. Staff and students seemed pleased to see me, but I think they were just pleased to see anyone from the outside world taking an interest in them.

On the last day they held a service of thanksgiving service in my honour, presenting me with an intricate hand-made wooden plaque that depicted my visit. In my head I can still hear their beautiful, unaccompanied, hymn singing. When I got back to my room in the house that afternoon, I could not hold back the tears. That evening they drove me back to the airport, and the heavens opened with an equatorial rain storm. It seemed appropriate.

Back in England I quickly got back into the routine of work and home, but a couple of weeks later I was sitting on a plane to Dublin and staring down at the floor, when I noticed that the cracks of my shoes were still filled with red dust. It lightened my mood to realise that I had brought a tiny bit of Liberia back home with me. And then I thought that that was only fair, because I think I left a tiny bit of myself over there.

VIII

Forty shades of Green

Ballycroy 7 – that was the full telephone number. Not that I could dial it directly from the UK - in the early 1980s I still had to book a call with the Irish Operator, and wait for a call back when a line became available. Even then I would still only be as far as the village postmistress. 'You're after Frank, is it? Well you won't be getting him this afternoon – he's usually out for a walk on Wednesday afternoons.' I got the distinct impression that when I eventually got through, she would be monitoring the conversation.

I was calling to take up his offer to go and stay with him for a few days. I'd never stayed in Ireland before, and, come to that, I'd never actually met Frank, though I'd corresponded with him for a few years. He was an early subscriber, and later a regular contributor, to the computer magazine that I'd co-founded while at university. He was clearly a very interesting and erudite man: our correspondence touched on an eclectic range of subjects. I gathered he was an American citizen, but of Irish descent, and had retired to County Mayo, on the rugged west coast of Ireland.

I drove off the ferry at Rosslare before 7 am, and climbed the hill away from the harbour. I faced a long drive diagonally across the country, but the road was empty and I decided to get some miles under my belt before the traffic began. Irish people sometimes describe their countryside as being 'forty shades of green' and as I started to drive across the country I could see why.

The traffic never did begin, and I had one of the most enjoyable day's driving of my life. I had just bought a beautiful white Porsche 928S that had previously belonged to the tennis player David Lloyd. The roads were wide, the corners smooth, and the visibility excellent. If there were any Gardaí (the Irish police) on the roads they either didn't see me, or perhaps they just couldn't keep up.

I finally got to Ballycroy and managed to triangulate various confusing instructions from the locals - 'keep going until you get to a T-junction, then go straight over,'– and drove down a long drive to Frank's house.

Frank turned out to be even more delightful and interesting in person than as a correspondent. We played a large range of board games, from Othello to the Japanese game of Go. He won most of them, though relying heavily on subterfuge and deception, it seemed to me. It transpired that he was a longstanding member of the Magic Circle, and a paid up member of the Sceptics.

One of his many hobbies was ornamental turning and machining, and he used these skills to create wonderfully complex mechanical puzzles. I would spend an hour trying to find out how to open one of his puzzle boxes, pushing and pulling on every obvious affordance: only to discover that if I just turned it over the top would twist off easily. Each year he would go to an international conference to meet other puzzle makers, and make exchanges.

Some years later he told me that he had finally acquired a puzzle he had coveted for years (I had the impression we were talking thousands of pounds worth). He described it as a small-scale chest of drawers, made from finely carved wood and brass, about eight inches tall. The challenge was to open the top drawer to reveal the treasure inside, and Frank said it was designed by someone with 'a mind even dirtier than mine!' There were thirty-two separate steps to solving the puzzle - the first step alone was to unscrew all four of the small scale turned-brass feet, and then screw them back on again in a different order ...

When we weren't playing games, solving puzzles, or discussing a huge range of books, we walked in the local countryside. Frank's house was set in 300 acres of rugged coastline and ornamental woodland. It had been built in the 19th century as the shooting lodge for a large European-owned estate. Frank's father had bought it in a dilapidated state just after the Second World War. It originally had a balcony running around the upper story, providing an alternative route between bedrooms for clandestine liaisons, but it had decayed so much that he'd had to remove it.

With Irish independence in 1922, the bulk of the estate had been confiscated, but the then owner had managed to retain the exclusive shooting and salmon fishing rights over 30,000 acres – which was where most of the value lay. Frank couldn't afford to maintain a gamekeeper or a ghillie, but he had a convenient arrangement with the local Gardaí, who all fished there for free and provided an effective deterrent to poachers. Rural Ireland is, as they say, 'a law unto itself'.

A former colleague of mine spent several boyhood summers on his cousins' farm in that same part of the world. On one occasion his cousins' parents were going away for the weekend, leaving the boys to fend for themselves. They hatched a plot to drive the parents'

31

other car into the nearest town for an evening of merriment; they were all well below the legal driving age, but had been driving tractors around the fields for years. But after the initial enthusiasm, they began to get cold feet, worrying about the consequences of getting caught.

Then they had a brilliant idea: they would phone the local guard, who they'd known for years, and ask his advice. 'Yes, boys, I see the dilemma,' said the policeman, 'You don't want to be wasting the opportunity, but I can't have you driving a car in my town underage. So here's what I suggest: just before the bridge over the river there's a lay-by with a telephone box. Park there, and call me. I'll come and meet you there and drive you the last mile into town. Then at the end of the evening you can call me again and I'll drop you back at your car over the bridge. That way everybody's happy.'

There's something wonderful about that story. I don't know whether I'm struck most by the reaction of the policeman, or by the innocence of the boys in deciding to ask his advice about breaking the law.

IX

Unfolding the design

A handful of the books in my library are so precious to me – in terms of content, that is, not market value – that I keep two copies: one that I may occasionally lend to other people, and a back-up copy to ensure that I am never without access to it. One of those books is Christopher Alexander's *A Pattern Language*.

I came across his work by accident. I was searching for the source of a delicious quotation - 'Carve the problem at its natural joints, not mangling the parts like an unskilful butcher' - and had seen a reference attributing it to one of his books (wherein I learned that the original source was actually Plato's *Phaedrus*). But the almost poetic beauty of Alexander's writing about design in general, and architecture in particular, captured my imagination, and I quickly progressed to his others.

A Pattern Language is the best known, and the most practicable. He and his co-authors define some 253 patterns for building, from small-scale wooden detailing, to the layout of entire towns and cities. These specific patterns, they argue, define environments in which people feel naturally comfortable. You might say that this idea shares some qualities with the Chinese philosophy of *Feng Shui*, but *A Pattern Language* does not embody any form of mysticism, it is based purely on geometry. That distinction, incidentally, has not prevented Alexander from acquiring an almost cult-like following around the globe; Prince Charles is known to be a fan. But many of the big-name contemporary architects feel the same way about him as he does about them: they detest each other. His theoretical approach, and the many buildings that he has personally designed, are the antithesis of modernism, not because they hark back to classical styles (though one senses that he is more comfortable with those than with recent trends) but because his designs are 'organic'. Even that term needs qualifying: it is not in the sense of green politics and 'sustainability', but in the sense of being human scaled and full of life.

For years it was my ambition to design my own house, and when the opportunity arose in 2000, I was determined to apply all that I had learned from his books. I think it is possible to observe more than 40 of his design patterns in our home. Every room has natural light from two sides; the window recesses ('reveals') are not squared-off but angled to soften the light; and the outdoor spaces have a positive shape – to name but three.

It is not sufficient just to apply these specific patterns. For a building to have this 'quality without a name' it is necessary that the design process be also organic in nature. He talks about the design 'unfolding' - you must start by identifying the best location on the site and then put the most important room of the house (in our case, the kitchen) in that place. Next you must design the journey from the road into that space - which should be direct, symmetrical if possible, and with a sense of closing down and then opening up. Moving away from that primary space there should be a 'gradient of intimacy' - how far a guest moves from that centre reflects their degree of familiarity. And so on ...

34

His ideas have been applied, and sometimes mis-applied, to a wide range of other fields, from art and music, to science, even religion. In the computer science section of my bookshelves I have several books on re-usable patterns for software design that cite his work as an inspiration. Alexander himself, though, who understands much more about their field than he generally lets on, has been quite scathing about some of these 'applications' of his ideas, which he feels have missed the fundamental message. A book of re-usable architectural patterns is hardly a new idea: Andrea Palladio had done that in 1580 with his *Four Books of Architecture*, itself an echo of Vitruvius' *Ten Books of Architecture* in the first century BC. Alexander was striving for something much deeper – understanding the very nature of order.

However, it was because of his following in the software world that I came to meet him, in 2003. Chris, as I now know him, had been invited to give a keynote speech at a TTI Vanguard conference in San Diego. These conferences are very exclusive - you can't just buy a ticket, you need to be a subscribing corporate member, and that costs serious money. But I had spoken at Vanguard a couple of times, so I called up the organiser and asked if she would let me attend the first day as a guest, just to listen to the keynote. To be honest, I knew from watching a video that he is not a great speaker – it's not his medium – but as a devotee I just wanted to hear some of his messages from his own mouth. I flew to San Diego at my own expense just for the privilege.

On the opening morning of the conference, I arrived at the buffet breakfast and recognised Chris immediately. I introduced myself and asked if he would sign my copy of *A Pattern Language*, which he graciously did. But I could tell he was not at ease and did not want to get into conversation – I've been that way myself before a big speech – so I left him alone and sat down in the conference room. Ten minutes before the start, the organiser sought me out: they had a problem. Chris was due to be introduced by Nicholas Negroponte (the then Director of the Media Lab at MIT, and author of the best-selling *Being Digital*) but Nicholas was ill, and none of the other faculty really knew much about Chris. Would I be willing to introduce him? Would I be willing to introduce one of my all-time heroes at one of the most prestigious conferences in the world? You bet I would.

Hurriedly, I composed an introduction. I have long ranted about how badly speakers are often introduced and I wasn't going to make the same mistake. When the moment came, I briefly described his work, its huge significance, and its impact on my own thinking; and then I took a risk. 'I predict two things,' I said, 'The first is that he will break every rule of good presentation style; the second is that he will leave you utterly transfixed.' Both predictions came good.

An hour later, when the chairman announced a coffee break, Chris came bounding up to me, beaming, his whole demeanour different than at our earlier encounter. 'I can't thank you enough for that introduction. It made a huge difference.' He invited me to join him for dinner that evening. Several weeks later, I received an email inviting me to stay with him at his home in Sussex.

There we spent hours exploring ideas. Mostly it was me learning from him, but I was able to introduce him to a couple of new ideas which clearly took root with him. One of them was the work of Aristid Lindenmayer, the first person to identify a simple mathematical formula that could, for example, distinguish the shape of an oak tree from a beech tree, for example. The key idea, which

Chris latched onto straight away, was that the best way to model the final shape of a tree, was to model the way that it grew. The sophisticated computer-generated 'natural' scenery now widely used in feature films is all derived from Lindenmayer's work.

But on that visit I learned much more about Chris the person, in part from him, and in part from his elderly father who was also living in the house. Chris had been a bright pupil at school and won a scholarship to Cambridge, where he wanted to study architecture. But Cambridge offered only a Bachelor's degree in Architecture and his father insisted that he take a subject that would result in a Masters. So Chris opted for Mathematics, later adding a BA in Architecture for good measure.

From Cambridge he went to Harvard, and was awarded the first PhD in Architecture by that institution. When he submitted his thesis (later published as his first book *Notes on the Synthesis of Form*) the small Harvard Architecture faculty didn't know what to make of it - it bore no resemblance to any previous body of work and managed to be both poetic in style and mathematical in content. After sitting on it for months they eventually decided to refer it to the more technical minds at MIT, where it came to the attention of Marvin Minsky, co-founder of the MIT Artificial Intelligence laboratory, and widely regarded as one of the finest minds of a generation. (While writing this very paragraph I looked up Minsky's details online and discovered that he'd just died this week). A couple of weeks later Minsky sent the thesis back to Harvard with a note scrawled on the front: 'I think you had better award this young man his PhD straight away, to save Harvard from future embarrassment.'

X

Faster than the sun

My colleague, Rob, lived five miles due west from me, and it just happened that we would often be talking on the phone mid-morning, which meant that he would identify the noise via the telephone, a few seconds before hearing it directly.

'Concorde.'

The noise was supposed to be one of the issues that limited its take-up by the airlines, but I loved the sound; it wasn't really very loud, but it was certainly distinctive, a low continuous rumble. I loved Concorde's elegant shape even more. My house, near Henley on Thames, backs onto an open field and it afforded an uninterrupted view of Concorde's flight path from shortly after take-off, to somewhere west of Reading, following the shortest route to the Bristol Channel. On the days when I wasn't talking to Rob at exactly 11.05, on hearing the rumble I would go out onto the patio and watch the full traverse of this graceful bird; and again at 7.05 in the evening. At certain times of the year its flight into the setting sun was sublime.

On the day of its final flight in 2003 I held a drinks party on the patio for like-minded friends; we drank Champagne, like those on board would be doing, and watched the aircraft fly past us, a sadness hanging in the air. Some years later the television presenter Jeremy Clarkson took a flight on a 747 to New York. 'Imagine that,' he said to camera, 'London to New York in seven and a half hours. In my day it was three and a half.' Like the Apollo moon-shots there is that sense of having lost a technology that we once had.

Despite the periodic news items announcing some boffin's idea for a hypersonic space-plane that will offer London to Melbourne in a couple of hours, I very much doubt that any such project will get off the ground, literally or even figuratively - it will be killed off by all the same factors that worked against Concorde's success. By no stretch of the imagination was Concorde a commercial success, yet I don't know any British man that doesn't think it was worth the huge cost to the taxpayer of its development. It was our nearest equivalent to Apollo space program in more ways than one.

The physical experience of travelling on Concorde was insignificant - the plane was cramped and noisy, and the windows so tiny you could barely see out. As it crossed the coast at Bristol the captain would announce that he was switching on the 'reheats' (afterburners), in pairs, 'There go the outer pair ... and there go the inner pair'. With each pair you could fee a slight push in the back as the additional thrust kicked in, but if it wasn't for the announcement and the digital Mach-meter display at the front of the passenger cabin, you would have no sense of going supersonic.

The most striking thing was that once you'd drunk your post take-off glass of champagne, followed by a pretty good four course meal, coffee and liqueur, the captain would announce, 'We will shortly be commencing our descent into New York'.

On my last flight on Concorde, shortly after commenc-ing the descent, the Cabin Services Director made his announcement of preparations for landing, ending with, 'As usual for a night-time landing, we will be dimming the cabin lights – but you may continue to use the individual reading lights if you wish'. Then, departing from the standard script, he continued, 'I'll be dimming them in pairs. There go the outer pair ... and there go the inner pair,' neatly parodying the earlier words of the captain.

For me, nothing better encapsulates the best of the British spirit than that little event. Invent (all right, co-invent, with the French) the world's fastest, most technologically sophisticated, and most beautiful passenger plane ever built, but then don't then take yourselves *too* seriously.

XI

Solution

The man was manipulating something in his hands; it was brightly coloured, but from the distance of perhaps 20 yards, Tom couldn't make out what it was. Yet even from that distance, something didn't look quite right about it - what the man was doing to it almost didn't seem physically possible. As Tom described it to me many years later, some neuron in his brain fired, telling him that he was observing something of significance. Within a couple of years of that encounter, Tom would become a very wealthy man.

The device that the man was manipulating was called the Magic Cube. Later, it would be re-named, taking on the surname of its inventor: Erno Rubik. A lecturer in design, Rubik had created the first prototype purely as an exercise in design, to prove that it was possible to create a cube where all six sides could be fully rotated without the pieces falling apart. (The idea that it could also be a puzzle came later.) It is difficult now for most people to imagine, or recall, just how impossible that seemed when you first saw it in operation; this was what caused the neuron to fire in Tom's brain.

A small number of the devices had been sold within Hungary, but Tom believed that this device had much greater potential, and somehow negotiated the rights to license it to major toy manufacturers around the world. It would eventually become the world's best-selling toy – ever. In retrospect, like many ultimately popular ideas, its success seems pre-destined; at the time, however, that was far from obvious.

Tom took the cube to every major toy company in the world (most of which are American), and not one was interested in licensing it. Simple, generic puzzles, such as solitaire, had an enduring appeal, but they could not command the revenues or profits that would attract a major toy company. At the other extreme, there was a market for fiendishly-complex puzzles, but it was tiny.

To add to that, it wasn't even clear back in 1979 that Rubik's cube *was* solvable. If you knew the exact sequence of moves that had taken a given cube from its 'virgin' state (each side having a uniform colour) to a scrambled state, then those moves could obviously be reversed in sequence. But if you didn't have access to that list of moves, or more likely, you had scrambled the cube yourself and not bothered to note them down, then how could you work out what to do? Just possibly the cube was like one of those 'trapdoor' codes that form the basis of modern cryptography, whereby making public the simple knowledge of how to encrypt a message does not give them the ability to decrypt it. When Ideal Toys eventually decided to take a gamble on the cube (the company was near to bankruptcy and figured it had little to lose with one last big punt), Tom was required to guarantee that the cube could in fact be solved. Incredibly, Tom at one point proposed that Ideal should put up a prize of one million dollars to the first person who could solve a cube in an hour. That never happened, but when I bought my first cube in in 1980, the department store initially offered a cash prize if you could solve it in 10 minutes; no one did.

Many of my friends had bought cubes, but none could solve it, though most could get one whole face of the cube to a uniform colour. I had the idea of writing a software tool, not to solve the cube (I couldn't conceive how to do that) but to act as a sort of helper to someone, brighter than I, who might be able to do it. First, I would need a concise notation for representing the state of the cube, and each of the moves. Next I had the idea of memorising a sequence of simple moves as a compound move, and then compounding the compound moves. I envisaged managing a small library of those moves, each with a name, and a succinct definition of its net impact on each piece in the cube.

I never got as far as writing a working version of this program, because in the course of designing it on paper and experimenting with the notations, I realised that I was actually beginning to solve the cube for myself. Very quickly I was able to get to two complete layers of colour, and once I'd established the pattern, in less than a week I'd found a complete solution. I rushed back to the shop and demonstrated that I could solve the cube; sadly it took me more than 10 minutes.

I learned, again, the invaluable principle that if you can't figure out how to solve a whole problem, try to solve just a small part of it because this might well lead to an insight on how to solve the next part, and so on. More specifically, to echo the words of Herb Simon, a renowned expert on Artificial Intelligence and other computational techniques, the essence of problem solving is largely about changing the representation of the problem until the solution becomes obvious.

Even in 1980 I was far from the only person who'd figured it out, but one of a fairly select group. A couple of weeks later *Der Spiegel* published a complete solution, very similar to the one I'd found, and within a few weeks everyone who'd bought a cube could solve it. The challenge then moved on to finding more efficient algorithms, and eventually to solving the cube in seconds rather than minutes.

I met Tom Kremer in 1985 and we did some business together. On a long flight from Tokyo to Los Angeles, relaxing in First Class (sadly, such luxuries are just a distant memory for me now), I learned some of the more personal side of his life story.

Tom was born in Transylvania, into a Jewish family. He and his parents were rounded up by the Nazis during the war and sent to the Bergen Belsen concentration camp. Unusually, they all survived. They were among the group of 1684 rescued from the camp, by the negotiations of a Hungarian Jew named Rudolf Kastner and sent to Switzerland on a single train - a story that has some parallels to that of Schindler's List, though is less well known. It is a story not without controversy - in 1957 Kastner was publicly accused in Israel of having collaborated with the Nazis, and was assassinated by a group of right-ring Israeli activists. The following year the supreme court of Israel cleared his name.

As a result of the whole experience, Tom became an ardent Zionist, and immediately after the war de-camped to Palestine, ultimately joining the Haganah to fight in the Israeli war of independence in 1948. Later he moved to Rhodesia, and then to Britain, to study Philosophy at Edinburgh University, where he met Alison, whom he would later marry.

The Israeli War of Independence, in which Tom fought, was the culmination of a process that had started in 1917 with the Balfour Declaration, a letter sent by the Earl of Balfour, as Foreign Secretary in the British

46

Government, to Baron Rothschild, as a representative of British Jewry, confirming the support of His Majesty's government for the establishment of a homeland for the Jews in Palestine. The Balfour Declaration is still controversial. Was Britain right or wrong to have made this declaration at all? Did other territorial promises made by Britain, to the French, and to the Arabs, conflict with the Balfour Declaration, or not? Whether right or wrong, did Britain honour the commitment, or renege on it? What had been Britain's real motivation? Was a peaceful outcome ever a possibility? I have read many books on this; each one has answered at least one outstanding question, and raised perhaps three more. Unlike Rubik's cube, there is, as yet, no credible solution to the problem of Israel/Palestine.

Arthur Balfour died in 1930, while Palestine was still ruled by Britain under a mandate from the League of Nations, before the full extent of Arab opposition to the plan had manifest itself, and before the Nazi attempted genocide of the Jewish people. He had no children, so the earldom passed to his brother, Gerald, who did have a family.

By an extraordinarily ironic coincidence, the Alison that Tom Kremer married, was - unbeknownst to him when they started dating - the second earl's granddaughter: Lady Alison Balfour.

XII

Peace like a river

'**S** aved'. The first word of the telegram raised his hopes. It was from his wife, so she had survived the accident. The second word dashed them: 'alone'. It meant that all four of their daughters were dead - drowned at sea.

The year was 1873. Horatio Spafford (pictured) was a lawyer and property investor in Chicago. The family had planned a tour of Europe, together with a couple of close friends. At the last minute, Horatio was detained on business, needing to sign some urgent papers. They decided that Anna and the four girls should proceed as planned, taking the steamship *Ville Du Havre* from Boston; Horatio would follow them a couple of days later to rendezvous in Paris. Off the coast of Newfoundland their ship collided with another vessel, the *Loch Earn*, and sank within 12 minutes. News of the disaster quickly reached Chicago, but Horatio had to wait an agonising three days for news of survivors. On receiving the telegram he boarded the next ship to France to be with this wife, and on board the ship, he penned these extraordinary words:

> *When peace like a river attendeth my way,*
> *when sorrows like sea billows roll;*

whatever my lot, thou hast taught me to say,
"It is well, it is well with my soul."

I have always loved singing this hymn (it has four more verses), and have known the outline of the story behind it since I was quite young - probably I heard my father tell it in the pulpit. I have rather mixed feelings about the words, though. On the one hand I deeply admire both the faith and the fortitude that Horatio demonstrated despite the tragedy; on the other hand I think there is something almost preternatural about his reaction. Yet over the years I have read much more detail about the incident, and about the lives of the Spafford family both before and afterwards, and found that my respect has grown steadily. For the drowning of their four daughters was not the first tragedy to befall them, and nor would it be the last.

Two years before the sinking they had lost most of their property in the Great Fire of Chicago, though the fire stopped just short of their own residence. Rather than dwell on their own misfortunes, Horatio and Anna devoted their efforts to helping others who had suffered worse than they. The trip to Europe was intended as a well-earned break from two years of hard work serving their community.

After the loss of their four daughters, the Spaffords returned to Chicago and considered themselves fortunate to be young enough to have more children. Horatio junior was born in 1876, followed two years later by Bertha. But their son contracted scarlet fever and died, aged four - and now follows what is possibly the worst part of the story. The Spaffords retained their strong Christian faith throughout these tragedies, but they were increasingly shunned by members of their own

Presbyterian church, many of whom believed that all this misfortune must indicate some secret sinfulness on their part. When Horatio Junior died, some doubtless well-meaning, but deeply misguided, friend in the church suggested that she adopt young Bertha - to save her from a similar fate.

The Spaffords had had enough. They parted company with their church, and the following year moved to Jerusalem, where they were shortly blessed by the birth of another girl, Grace. In Jerusalem, with thirteen others from America they formed a community, devoting themselves to the service of the poor, sick and needy. They were to face serious opposition to their work, including and especially from their own American ambassador, of whom they had cause to make formal complaint to Washington. He and others saw them as a dangerous sect and made quite absurd accusations about their practices. Certainly, some of their beliefs were a little off the mainstream of the church, adopting a 'universalist' theology for example, but, importantly, one of their governing principles was they never sought to make converts, neither to their own specific beliefs, nor to the Christian religion in general. They saw their role solely as demonstrating the love of God through service to others, and drew no distinction between Christians (there were many Arab Christians in greater Syria, of which Jerusalem was then a part), 'Mohammedans', or Jews, in rendering their service. Their community was initially based in a building inside the old city, though they later bought a larger compound that had once been a Pasha's palace.

In 2007 Ann and I visited Israel, touring around on our own. In Jerusalem we booked into the American Colony Hotel, a very pleasant boutique hotel, apparently favoured by many statesmen over the years. At the time I booked it, I had no idea that this was that same former Pasha's palace, the home of the Spaffords - the 'American Colony' being their local moniker. We found the corridors of the hotel lined with black and white photographs of the Spaffords and their co-colonists, both at home and touring the region. The Spafford photographic library is today one of the richest records of life in Jerusalem from the 1880s through to the first world war, when they ran their home as a hospital for wounded soldiers - of both sides.

This unexpected personal encounter with the Spaffords' story would be the first of several. On another trip some years later, I was reading the memoirs of their eldest surviving daughter, Bertha, a fascinating account not only of the colony, but of life in that region in the late nineteenth and early twentieth centuries. Between two other scheduled stops, our guide decided to show us the Jerusalem House of Prayer, a beautiful old stone house set in a tranquil garden, where pilgrims stop to pray or meditate. Unbeknownst both to the guide and to me, it transpired that this very house had been Bertha Spafford's own, after she had married and lived apart from her parents.

But the most extraordinary crossing of my path with that of the Spaffords occurred in 2003, in Bath, England, as the climax of a story that is unusual in almost every dimension. It starts with the scandalous collapse of Enron in the USA. In Britain the Wessex Water utility company that had been part of Enron was acquired by the YTL Corporation, a conglomerate of utilities, hotels, and construction companies across the globe, owned by a Malaysian Chinese family. The Chief Executive of YTL, Francis Yeoh, is an opera buff, and every year hosts a private concert featuring many of the world's top opera singers. To celebrate the acquisition of Wessex Water, he decided to hold his 2003 concert in Bath (their headquarters), and to make it free to the public. He arranged with Bath City Council to host the concert outdoors, directly in front of the magnificent Georgian Royal Crescent. In addition to giving away most of the 10,000 seats to the public by lottery, overflow screens and sound would be provided in the adjoining park to permit thousands more to enjoy the show. The three tenors - Luicano Pavarotti, José Carreras, and Placido Domingo - would all be performing.

Francis Yeoh is a Christian, and wears his faith very publicly on his sleeve – which is a brave thing to do in Malaysia, incidentally. It so happens that *It is well with my soul* is his favourite hymn, and he persuaded the three tenors to include it in their programme in Bath. Francis is also a fan of my father's preaching, and invited my father to sit next to him as his guest of honour on the front row. He also gave my father a number of reserved tickets to give to friends and family – which is how Ann and I came to hear The Three Tenors sing one of my favourite hymns.

Francis learned of the story behind the hymn only after he'd set up the concert. Moved by the story, he wondered if there were any known descendants. He managed to trace one, a grand-daughter of Bertha Spafford. Her name is Djemila, properly, Lady Djemila Cope of Berkeley: a village not far from Bath, where the concert was to be held. Francis invited her also as his personal guest.

The concert was so magical than no-one wanted it to end. It was an uncharacteristically warm summer evening, with not a cloud in the azure sky - as Francis quipped in his welcoming address, it must have been that 'God himself wanted to watch the concert'.

Afterwards, we were introduced to Francis, who then invited us to a private dinner party with his extended family, the three tenors, and a few other guests, including Lady Djemila. I was able to tell her of my love for the hymn, and interest in her ancestral family's story. She gave me a facsimile copy of the original version of the hymn, handwritten by Horatio Spafford.

XIII

The day the universe changed

F or many British people, the voice of James Burke is as indelibly associated with the moon landings as those of the astronauts themselves. He was already gaining a name for himself in the late 1960s as a presenter of *Tomorrow's World*, the BBC's science and technology magazine programme, before becoming special reporter for the Apollo moon-shots.

Through the 1970s and '80s he would cement his reputation as the thinking man's thinking man, with a series on the ethics and social implications of science, *The Burke Special*, followed by several series of *Connections*, which explored the development of technologies and ideas throughout history.

But, for me at least, his *magnum opus* was the television series *The Day the Universe Changed*, first aired in 1985. Each of the seven programmes, and chapters in the accompanying book, focused on a particular point in history where a change in understanding of the world took root, with dramatic consequences for mankind in the years, decades, and centuries that followed. The title itself is clever. Did the universe change? Was it merely our perception that changed? Or did our changing perception actually change the universe? In the opening page of the book, Burke recounts the story of a student of Ludwig Wittgenstein who remarks that before Copernicus, people must have been pretty stupid to think that the earth was the centre of the universe and rest of the cosmos circled around it. Wittgenstein agrees, but says that it would be interesting to speculate how things might have looked to them if the earth really was the centre – his point being that it would have looked pretty similar.

I credit this series with teaching me to think, or at least to think more broadly and more critically than my rather narrow education had taught me thus far. Later I would go on to read many of the sources that Burke was presenting in popular form: Thomas Kuhn, Carl Popper, Paul Feyerabend, and more. I have never despised popularisations of recondite subjects if they are done well. Unfortunately in recent years the BBC has gotten cold feet about this approach, worrying that having obvious intellectuals like James Burke as presenters is 'talking down' to the man in the street; so everything must now either be presented by an expert who pretends to know nothing, or by a celebrity who actually knows nothing. But as the critic AA Gill put it so well, 'I don't mind being talked down to by someone I look up to. What I mind is being talked down to by someone I look down on.'

I met James Burke in the late 1990s, by when his television career was largely over. He was to give a talk at a small conference my company was running in Palm Springs. He'd asked that someone meet him at the airport, and I jumped at the opportunity. The hour I spent with him in the car to the hotel was hugely enjoyable. I was able to tell one of my heroes just how much I appreciated his work, and in return he shared with me lots of interesting ideas and personal stories. I'll repeat just one of the latter, which I have never seen in print.

James Burke wasn't supposed to provide the commentary for the first moon walk. For that historic event the BBC wanted a real heavyweight, Cliff Michelmore, who was the anchor-man throughout the extensive Apollo 11 coverage. The Eagle landed at 10:17pm British time; the astronauts were scheduled to sleep for several hours and then step onto the surface of the moon around 7.00am. Cliff Michelmore and much of the BBC crew went off to a party; James Burke stayed behind to man the fort. Within an hour rumours started to trickle in from Mission Control that the astronauts were unable to sleep - not a big surprise, surely - and that the moon walk was going to be brought forward. By the time this was confirmed, the BBC's senior anchor-man was rather the worse for wear from partying, and so James Burke got the task of commentating the first moonwalk by default. That was one small, swaying, step for Michelmore, one giant leap for James Burke's career.

XIV

Music of the Spheres

'The first time you see an opera, you either love it or hate it,' says the character played by Richard Gere in *Pretty Woman,* 'If you hate it, you can still learn to love it – but it will never be a part of your soul.' Though I like the sentiment, I'm not sure it's true. I saw my first opera, *Don Giovanni,* in 1993, and I neither loved nor hated it, though I have certainly grown to love opera since. But it was love at first sight for the venue where it was performed: Sydney Opera House.

Sydney Opera House is, for me, one of the best examples of 20th century architecture in the world, possibly *the* best. Paraphrasing Christopher Alexander, the first duty of an architect is not to design a building that is beautiful in itself, but rather one that will enhance the building's surroundings. The opera house is a rare example - the building would not be nearly as attractive in another environment, and Sydney Harbour would be poorer without it.

Indeed, it is now so iconic, that it seems hard to imagine Sydney Harbour without it. Yet, just 60 years ago it was the site of a distinctly un-aesthetic tram terminus. And the conception, design, and construction of the building were so beset by problems – technical, financial, and political – that its very existence is almost as unlikely as its form.

From conception to opening, the project took more than 25 years, a timespan exceeded perhaps only by some of the great European cathedrals.

Vitruvius, writing in the first century BC, tells of an ancient law established in the city of Ephesus to encourage architects of public buildings to work within a budget. If the final cost actually came within the architect's estimate then he should be awarded special honours; if the cost overran by up to 25% then the difference should be borne by the public purse; but if the cost should overrun by more than 25% then the architect should personally pay the difference. Fortunately for the Danish architect of the Opera House, Jørn Utzon, there was no such law in New South Wales - the original estimate was 7 million Australian dollars, the final cost was 102 million. The project faced repeated calls for its cancellation from sceptical government officials and other public figures. Yet compared to the impact that the building has had on the identity of Sydney, to locals and visitors alike – and likely will have for centuries to come – the cost seems almost trivial.

The engineering and construction challenges faced, and overcome, add a dimension to the story that, for me, magnify the purely aesthetic impact. Utzon won the international design competition with little more than a pencil sketch. The sweeping form of the roof, referred to variously as 'shells' or 'sails', was hand-drawn - it was not defined by any geometrical curve. This was a problem for the consulting engineers, Ove Arup. The strength of the roof could not be analysed using any mathematics or computer modelling techniques available at that time. Physical scale models provided only limited data, and suggested that the structure was very vulnerable to a single point of failure. Over three years from 1959 to 1962,

Arup and Utzon explored many different variants on the shape of the roof, and alternative construction techniques. The evolution of the final form – the variants explored are well documented – resembles a classical Darwinian illustration of the evolution of a shell-fish.

The final design adopts a spherical geometry. Although it is not immediately obvious, all of the roof parts form sections of a single sphere approximately 20 metres in diameter. Moreover, all the edges of those roof sections (except for those that form the ridges at the top) are great circles on that sphere. This breakthrough not only facilitated the structural analysis, it also made the construction feasible. The whole roof is made up of more than 2000 pre-cast concrete sections, cast on site and then post-tensioned with steel cables for strength.

When I first read about this, I found the story of the changing geometry of the sails intriguing, if rather difficult to comprehend. I decided that the only way to get to get to grips with it was to attempt to build a scale model from scratch, as Utzon himself had done. Knowing that the all the sails formed sections of the same sphere, I decided to create them from sheets of modelling clay, rolled out as thin as I could manage (about 2.5 mm), and then mould them over a spherical former, leaving them to harden naturally. For the scale I wanted to work on, I needed a sphere about 30cm in diameter, and one day my gaze settled on an old globe that we had bought years earlier to encourage our children to learn about our many travels together. It was the perfect diameter, and I realized that it had another huge advantage: it was already marked out with latitude and longitude. From Utzon's complex diagrams, I could work out the angle subtended by each arc, and from this I could calculate the relative spherical coordinates of the three corners of each sail.

But there was a snag: on my globe, mountain ranges were depicted in low relief, so the only smooth parts were the ocean, and the only parts of the ocean large enough for my purposes are in southern hemisphere. I needed a specific edge of each sail – the one where it joins its matching partner to make the roof ridge – to be on a line of latitude so that I could make the cut parallel to the equator, using the frame of the rotating globe as a tool guide. After a few experiments, discovering the hard way that I needed to lubricate the surface of the globe with olive oil before smoothing out the ultra-thin clay on it and then trimming the edges, the end result was perfect. I never got around to completing the whole base of the model, but I had a perfect set of sails. I finally understood Utzon's insight.

And I've done something that Utzon never did: I've seen the finished building. He sadly fell out with his customer in 1966. It has been wrongly stated by some that this was to do with the changing shape of the exterior, but this is not the case - Utzon was quite happy with the final external form. The disagreement was more to do with the internals, both form and function. Utzon resigned from the project in 1966. Late in his life, he was reported to have finally come to terms with the differences, became reconciled, from a distance, with his antagonists, and expressed his satisfaction with the building as it stood. But by then he felt he was too old to travel to Australia. He died in 2008 having never viewed the finished building.

XV

Prometheus Unbound

'It was already one in the morning; the rain pattered dismally against the panes, and my candle was nearly burnt out, when, by the glimmer of the half-extinguished light, I saw the dull yellow eye of the creature open; it breathed hard, and a convulsive motion agitated its limbs.' I still get shivers when I re-read this wonderful passage from *Frankenstein*.

This classic book was written by an 18 year old girl, as her entry to an informal competition among a group of house guests on the shores of Lake Geneva (Lord Byron was another) - to see who could write the best horror story. Her name was Mary Godwin, but the book would initially be published anonymously. By the time she attached her name to it, she had changed it to Mary Shelley, taking the surname of her new husband, the poet.

Frankenstein is much more than a horror story, though. As its full title - *Frankenstein: or, the modern Prometheus* - suggests, its real theme is the quest for creating life. This is a recurring theme in mythology, literature, and films, from the original *Prometheus*, through the golems of medieval Jewish kabbalism, to *2001 a Space Odyssey* and *Blade Runner*. The motivation for the quest varies - scientific curiosity, commercial exploitation, or protection from enemies – but the eventual outcome is always the same: the creature turns on its creator.

In recent times, the pursuit of artificial life has shifted from fiction to science. 'Artificial Intelligence' or 'AI', a term coined by John McCarthy at MIT in 1955, is now a major branch of Computer Science, and Artificial Life is a recognised discipline within that, exploring both 'soft' life forms (autonomous agents within a virtual or simulated world), and hard forms (robots).

In 1985 I designed what I believe was the world's first fully-autonomous robot pet, called Scamp. There were already quite sophisticated robot toys on the market by the mid '80s, some even covered with plush to look like pet creatures. But all of them were effectively just remote-control devices - you either directed their movements live with a remote controller, or programmed them to execute a sequence of instructions. I was aiming for fully autonomous operation - a toy that a child could interact with, even influence, but never control. Indeed Scamp would continue to move around for a while even after the child had stopped playing with it – a favourite trope of children's literature. Your mother's question, when you couldn't find a toy, 'Where did you last have it?' would have no relevance.

Making a toy robot that could move around, make animated gestures, avoid obstacles, and sense various things about the environment was the easy part; the hard part was how to determine *what* it should do. I conceived the idea of a 'personality model' – Scamp's name actually stood for Self-Contained Autonomous Mobile with Personality. I now know that the model I came up with is similar to what psychologists call 'drive-based behaviour'. Scamp's software modelled a dozen different drives:

64

hunger, fatigue, irritation, curiosity, affection, boredom, and so on. Everything that Scamp sensed in the environment, including the passage of time, would potentially increment or decrement one or more of these drives, in different ways. The highest, or 'dominant' drive would trigger a behaviour that, directly or indirectly, would tend to reduce that drive. Thus, hunger would increase over time, faster in daylight than at night, and when hunger dominated the other drives, Scamp would search for food. Any energetic activity on Scamp's part would gradually add to fatigue, and when this became dominant, Scamp would exhibit gestures of fatigue, and eventually fall asleep. Repeated sequences of stimulation could increase Scamp's playfulness, but if fatigue was high then the same repeated stimulation could lead to increased irritation, and if that drive was dominant Scamp would 'bristle'. But while a person might observe the primary behaviour, they had no direct indication of the level of the drive that was causing it, or, importantly, of the other drives that were rising or falling – though small cues could be picked up from occasional gestures of the head or eyes.

Incidentally, the head moved on two axes, and the eyelids opened and closed by degrees, but the eyes never actually moved. Yet, as I would discover, several observers mentioned the movement of the eyes, or changing facial expressions, despite the fact that both were fixed. I discovered what many special effects specialists, not to mention conjurors, know: that once you cross a certain threshold of credibility, people will fill in huge amounts of detail for you.

Designing Scamp's personality took a lot of experimentation. We (the small team of robot engineers that I employed) designed some sophisticated software tools for specifying and editing the personality; the tools were collectively known as PROSE – Personal Robot Operating System and Environment. Initially, most of the code ran on a PC, where we could monitor all the activity on a screen display, and which was connected to Scamp via an umbilical cable; gradually, we transferred more of the functionality onto Scamp's built-in microprocessor. We saw ourselves only as designers and engineers, trying to create a really unique toy; we didn't get too philosophical about the artificial life idea. Yet I can recall with vivid clarity the moment when we discovered that we could cut the umbilical cord. It was a very weird sensation - not only was Scamp now operating autonomously, but we no longer had sight of its (his? her?) internal state, we could only observe the external behaviour.

With the help of our agent, Tom Kremer, we sought to license Scamp to a toy manufacturer. I'll never forget the presentation to Hasbro, the then largest toy company in the world. The senior executives in the room were bowled over. As I hinted earlier, what they thought they saw Scamp do and what it actually did were not entirely the same – but selling 'magic' is their business, and as the saying goes, there's no easier person to sell to than a salesman. We walked out of that meeting with the largest advance on royalties that they had ever signed, and a contract to develop the prototype further. For the next 12 months they flew me regularly to the USA and to Japan, for discussions with one of their manufacturing partners.

Sadly, Scamp never came to market. I have the only fully-working prototype in my attic. Some technical problems that, with hindsight, we could have managed better, and some politics within the company, high development costs, and a downturn in the toy market, that we couldn't have managed, resulted in the cancellation of

the project. Within a couple of years my robot company had become unsustainable, and I moved back into the more prosaic world of business information systems.

Scamp made one more public appearance. In 1988 I was invited to appear with Scamp, live, on the BBC with Terry Wogan (pictured). The well-known adage in television that you should never perform with animals or children should perhaps be extended to include robots; Scamp refused to play, and decided to wander off the set to explore the camera rostrum, with Terry Wogan crawling after it. The results are quite amusing, and may still be viewed on YouTube[1]. Incidentally, one of the other guests was a 13-year old English schoolboy, who had just starred in his first film: Christian Bale.

As I am writing this very piece, Ann comes in to say that she has just heard on the radio that Terry Wogan died this morning. He will be much missed. As one commentator has put it: 'if the Queen, a known fan, is the centre of gravity for the country, Terry Wogan was the centre of levity.'

Within a couple of years of ceasing work on Scamp, though, I had discovered an alternative mechanism for producing life, one that, for my part, involved a minimum of effort, though rather more on the part of my wife. The two successful products of these endeavours continue to bring us much joy and happiness.

---

[1] youtube.com/watch?v=u8ZEUwwOYxo

XVI

Reserve

'What happens now?' I asked our guide, as the last trace of the blood-red sun sank below the horizon. 'I thought we might try and find that lion,' he replied. 'What lion?' 'The one you can hear roaring just over there'. Suddenly, the idea of standing around in the open steppe, drinking sundowners, didn't seem quite so appealing; I gently ushered the family back onto the Land Rover. Not that I had heard any sound. I learned that night that a lion's roar isn't like the one from the MGM logo at the start of a film - it can be a gentle, almost subsonic, purr. Now that he'd mentioned it, I could just hear something. Despite the rapidly fading light, it seemed that our evening wasn't over yet.

Our guide, named Grant, drove around in the undergrowth for about half an hour, exchanging occasional syllables with Elvis, our African tracker, sitting next to him. I started to think that it was a charade, that we had about as much of a chance of a finding a lion in the by now pitch darkness, as of finding our tracker's namesake.

But then he stopped the Land Rover, turned off the engine, and turned on a powerful flashlight. Standing not twenty yards to the side of us, was a lioness. Twenty yards, that is, from the open sided Land Rover where we sat - with Guy and Aruna, aged eight and five. We'd had to get special permission to take Aruna on the drive, and I was beginning to hope that my assurance to the camp manager that she could be depended upon to behave, was accurate. I looked across at both the children - they were not showing any signs of fear, just wonderment. I was a just pondering the difference between Grant's conception of a safe distance and mine, when the lion started walking towards us – right up to the side of the Land Rover. I am not exaggerating when I say that Ann could have put down her hand and stroked the lioness, though it would have been the last thing she - Ann that is – would have done in this world. The lioness walked on by, apparently uninterested in us. Grant had warned us only that we should not stand up in the vehicle. I looked at Guy sitting next to me; he'd taken out his very small penknife and opened the blade, ready to defend us all.

We were on our first safari drive at the Londolozi game reserve, just off the Kruger National Park in South Africa. We'd only been out a couple of hours but we'd already seen a leopard guarding its recent kill up a tree, and a mother, father and baby rhinoceros trotting in line horn-to-tail (I imagine that the lead rhinoceros learns quite early on not to stop too suddenly). Within twenty four hours we'd have seen all the big five.

From the moment we arrived at Londolozi the whole experience was magical. As we approached the landing strip in the light aircraft, we passed over elephants bathing in the creek, and we saw the Land Rover speeding down the airstrip to meet us right off the plane.

The drives took place each evening and morning, starting before sun-up, when it was still bitingly cold. During the heat of the day we relaxed in our five-star 'huts' back at camp, phoning for an armed guard to escort us to the dining areas for the excellent meals; it was not uncommon for wildlife to walk right through the camp at night, and the previous month they'd had a lion fall into the swimming pool. The last meal of the day was around a campfire in the 'boma', an outdoor dining area surrounded by a wooden palisade for protection.

We spent just four days on safari, two at Londolozi, and two at Ngala, but the experience was so intense that it felt like a much longer holiday, different in so many ways from our every-day lives. Yet not entirely ...

As we returned to the camp on our last morning, we were driving along a track through some sparse woodland. We rounded a corner and saw that our way was blocked by a young male elephant. He flared his ears wide, and began to trot towards us. Our guide explained that this was a 'mock charge' - such a young elephant would not follow through on the threat. A charge from an adult male was an altogether more serious affair, and he had more than once had to practice reversing a Land Rover at high speed. Sure enough, our young male stopped short of us, moved off into the trees to the side of us, and started foraging – pulling up young shoots with his trunk. Watching him closely through my binoculars, though, I noticed that none of the pickings were going into his mouth. Curious, I asked our guide what the elephant was doing. 'He's pretending to eat,' he laughed.

More than any other wild animal elephants demonstrate very human like emotions: in this case pride. The young elephant didn't want to admit that he had given way to us, so he was showing us that he'd only moved off the path because he wanted something to eat. In just a couple of minutes, Craig predicted, his foraging would conveniently end back on the track just behind us. I found myself musing on the idea of elephants going on safari to observe the social behaviour at an English boys' school, perhaps...

XVII

Mastery

'You've got a full tank of fuel,' said Vaughan, my instructor, 'so if you aren't happy with your approach just go around again, as many times as you need to. Off you go, and good luck!' My first solo flight.

The first two circuits went smoothly: take-off, ascend, turn down-wind, descend, land, taxi, take-off again ... On the third loop, I noticed that the trees beyond the end of the runway seemed to have grown higher; either that or I was climbing more slowly ... I quickly discovered that I hadn't pushed the throttle fully open. I don't want to pretend it was a close thing - I was still well clear of the trees - but it was a salutary reminder of the need for care.

At least I had my hand on the throttle: during my first few lessons, I'd not always remembered. On one occasion, just 200 feet off the runway, in the corner of my eye I saw Vaughan reach over from the co-pilot's seat and pull back the throttle to idle. 'Why did you do that?' I yelled, just remembering to push the nose down (to avoid a stall) before slamming the throttle on full again to resume the climb. 'Do what?' he said, 'The throttle must have slipped. You should always have your hand on the throttle below 1000 feet.' I never made that mistake again.

Vaughan was a very good instructor, if sometimes a little unconventional, and this helped my confidence, even during the slightly scary experiences of deliberately induced stalls and spins. I recall only one collapse of confidence, and that was on the ground. We had finished the lesson and I was taxiing back to our parking place between two lines of light aircraft. With a wingspan of 28 feet, I was monitoring the clearance on either side carefully, but it seemed to me that the two lines were converging and I was getting nervous. Finally, I stopped the plane and asked him to take control. He muttered something to the effect that I was being pathetic, but he was also getting a little impatient. 'I have control,' he growled. 10 seconds later – bang! He'd hit the port wing tip on another plane. Fortunately, or unfortunately, depending on how you look at it, the plane he'd hit also belonged to him. Worse, it took place right outside the club house - I'm sure he would have attributed the collision to his student pilot.

I'd flown solo after just 10 hours of flying experience; I've since learned that it is not uncommon, but it still seems a remarkably short time to me. I doubt there are many people that have driven a *car* solo after 10 hours experience, at least not legally; when I learned to drive they reckoned that you needed a hour's lesson for each year of your life - further driving experience between lessons was encouraged but wasn't feasible for many young people.

A couple of years ago I spent Christmas in Australia staying with extended family. My nephew and niece were both learning to drive. Apparently, in Australia you need to have 120 hours of formally logged driving experience before you can take your test, which strikes me as very sensible given the accident rate of young drivers. While there I met a friend of my nephew, a charming young man in his early twenties. I was playing pool with him and only half concentrating on what he was saying - something about staying over ... parents away ... airline pilot. I made the embarrassing mistake of inferring that his dad was an airline pilot, and asked who he flew with; it turned out that it was the young man himself who was the airline pilot, a First Officer flying 767s overseas with a major low-cost airline. I apologised for my *faux pas*, and congratulated him on his achievement. 'Out of interest,' I asked, 'how many logged flying hours do you need to become a First Officer on a commercial jet?' '200.' For the second time in as many minutes I did a poor job of masking my surprise. It seems a very low figure in contrast to the 120 logged hours required to take a car test.

How long should it take to acquire a new skill? Popular management wisdom suggests that it takes 10,000 hours to become fully proficient in something. Winston Churchill famously said that when he got to heaven (not 'if', I note) he meant 'to spend a considerable portion of my first million years in painting, and so get to the bottom of the subject'.

By contrast, there's a great moment near the start of the science-fiction movie *The Matrix* where Trinity, running towards a helicopter with gunmen in hot pursuit, yells down her radio link to base, 'I need you to download me the skill to fly a helicopter - now!' Trinity is, in that scene, an avatar operating in a virtual world, so anything is possible, but I have worked with some extraordinary software developers who seem to have that capability for real. I have one friend who practically did that for flying real helicopters - by the end of his one-hour trial lesson, he'd managed a 360 degree turn while hovering. On my only helicopter lesson I managed to hold a hover for just a few seconds only, before the craft would lurch out of control, calmly restored each time by my instructor.

I never did enough hours to get my Private Pilot's Licence. Despite being young, single, and earning a good salary, funding the expense of a high performance car and flying lessons proved just too much. The car seemed the better option, even if it did have about the same fuel consumption as the plane; and offered similar odds on a premature death, I imagine.

My last flying lesson with Vaughan was a day trip to Guernsey. Not quite half-way across the English Channel, flying at 3000 feet, he pointed out of the window down at the sea. 'That's where I lost my other plane,' he said. Engine failure in a single-engine aircraft mid-channel is no laughing matter – he was well out of gliding range to any coast. He managed to transmit a Mayday call, and a search and rescue helicopter was dispatched. The plane hit the waves with some impact. His friend, another pilot, verified the story, and she had a small but deep scar on her forehead from where she'd hit the control column. Once down they scrambled out of the plane and into the life-raft, though not before rescuing the duty-free from the luggage compartment, apparently. I hope that last bit was a joke, because within two minutes of getting into the life-raft, the plane had sunk.

XVIII

Minimum

'And this is the dining room ... and this is the master bedroom.' You know how it is when people show you round their home: they can't help but explain what is completely obvious from the contents of the room. However a man once showed me around his house, where such an explanation was necessary, because despite his having lived there with his wife and young children for some years, most of the rooms contained almost nothing that would give away their function.

His name is John Pawson; given that our ancestors come from the same part of Yorkshire it seems likely that we are related, although we have not been able to establish a direct link. John is one of the most famous 'minimalist' architects in the world. I was introduced to him by a mutual friend, in part to give us the opportunity to find out if we were related, and in part because I wanted to learn more about Japanese culture in advance of my first visit there; John had lived there for a while, learning Japanese architecture and Zen philosophy, and the relationship between them.

We met at his apartment in fashionable south-west London, and he gave me the tour. Every room had the same décor - ebony-black wooden floors, and plain white walls, with no skirting boards, cornices, or even architraves around the doors. You might imagine that this had at least the benefit of economy, but apparently not - John explained that when you can't rely on wooden mouldings to cover the joins, the plastering has to be to a far higher standard.

The easiest room to identify was the sitting room, because it had a chair in it. Literally. The bedroom had no visible furnishings at all; each night they would bring out futons from hidden cupboards, the white doors of which were flush with the walls. The kitchen had an altar-like island in the middle, topped in polished black granite, with a low depression at one end serving as the sink; the tap, and the other appliances were well hidden.

I can't say the apartment was to my taste, but I do have some sympathy with the minimalist philosophy in design. One of my favourite quotations comes from Antoine de Saint-Exupéry: 'The design is completed, not when there is nothing more to add, but when there is nothing more to take away.' This principle was one of the driving forces that led to the idea embodied in my PhD thesis, *Naked Objects*, and when I subsequently started a company - Naked Objects Group - to apply the thesis commercially, we adopted that quotation as the official company motto.

I can also understand the idea that de-cluttering your physical environment is a step towards de-cluttering your mind. Some years ago I attended a lecture by the Himalayan mountaineer, Doug Scott, which he illustrated with some superb slide photography. He broke all the rules of good presentation technique - he sat on a stool in complete darkness, and talked in a monotonous voice. Yet it was gripping stuff, albeit magnificently under-stated. 'Had a bit of a fall on the way down and broke both my legs ... but was fortunately still able to crawl ... the food and water had both run out three days before ... but we found half a Mars bar in one of the rucksacks and the three of us feasted on that ...' Many of his slides featured other famous mountaineers with whom he had once climbed. This one had subsequently died from a cerebral oedema on Everest; that one in a fall on K2; those two in an avalanche in the Andes...

But what I remember most from the evening was his response to the inevitable question about what motivated him to take these risks. He said that following every climb in the Himalayas he would spend a couple of weeks camping in the warm valleys below, just recovering strength and health. In normal life, he said, your brain is crammed with thoughts; but he described just sitting there on the lakeshore at Pokhara where 'you would see a thought coming slowly up the valley from many miles away ... it would pass through your mind ... and then you'd watch it move slowly away down the valley.' Those moments were the reward.

John Pawson is clearly aiming for something similar in his architecture, though without the risk to life and limb of Himalayan climbing. I find it quite appealing, even if somewhat extreme. He told me that some years ago a Franciscan order of friars in what was then East Germany were looking for an architect to design them a new monastery. They came to view his work and liked what they saw, though they described some of his designs as 'just a little *too* austere.'

XIX

High Rise

The morning mist parted and suddenly they appeared, like two leviathans surfacing for air, side by side: the gigantic airship hangars at Cardington. One of the two hangars had been built to house the R101 airship, but the crash on its maiden overseas flight in 1930, killing 48 of the 54 people on board, ended British interest in rigid airships. Since then the hangars have been put to a variety of uses, from film studios to research into building construction.

I parked just outside the end-doors, so high and so heavy that they had to be pulled open by tractors - like the scene in Lord of the Rings, where the two captive trolls pull open the enormous gates to Mordor. I wondered when they had last been opened. I entered through a small side door. It was almost as foggy inside as out. I was later told that occasionally it can be raining inside the hanger even when it is not raining outside - the sheer height of the buildings allows clouds to form and become saturated within the roof void.

At the far end was a special building, constructed by the Building Research Establishment. Eight stories high, it was nonetheless all but lost within the scale of the hanger. My interest lay in a device that was currently clinging half-way up the glass 'curtain' wall on one side of that building.

Looking like a giant mechanical beetle, it was in fact an autonomous robot window cleaner. A press conference would commence shortly, giving the assembled journalists a chance to see the robot working for the first time.

The robot had been commissioned by the large cleaning services company, OCS Group, and built by their subsidiary, Cradle Runways, which makes many of the moving gantries that you see atop skyscrapers, from which the human window cleaners dangle precariously. The department of Robotics at Newcastle University had acted as specialist consultants for much of the project. But the original design idea for the robot was mine, and I had sold OCS the patent rights.

The idea of an automated window cleaning device was not original - the costs and hazards associated with high rise window cleaning make it an obvious target for the application of robotics. But all the existing designs that I knew about could not match the quality of manual cleaning. My idea was to try to mimic the technique used by a human window cleaner with a squeegee. The robot would first use a probe to measure the dimensions of each window frame and then plan and execute the twisting path for the squeegee, always angling the blade to keep the suds moving away from the cleaned surface.

To avoid the suds accumulating at the bottom we arranged for the cleaning head to vacuum them away from the squeegee blade as it moved. It was then a relatively small step to realise that we could have two squeegee blades a few millimetres apart, with the cleaning fluid both applied and retrieved between them. Many months of prototyping and experimentation were involved, but both the robot and the cleaning head ultimately proved to be very effective, and the demonstration in Cardington to assembled journalists was flawless.

The OCS prototype robot never became a commercial product. The limitation of my design was that the robot needed narrow guidance rails to ensure accuracy of movement, which limited it to new buildings. Even there commercial architects are notoriously reluctant to make design concessions for such mundane considerations as cleaning, which is why their elegant buildings often end up with an ugly gantry on top, applied as an afterthought.

However, the project was not entirely a waste of money for OCS. As well as affording some more interesting opportunities for publicity than those typically available to a cleaning services company, the research and development yielded a very useful spin-off technology: digital position control for conventional access gantries. On the strength of this technology, which none of their competitors had, the company secured a substantial contract for the refurbishment of the landmark Centre Point building in central London. Every time I walk past it, I look up at the gantry on top and think that it relies on something I invented.

That was twenty five years ago. Recently, I was in my local DIY superstore, when I noticed that Karcher, a leading manufacturer of pressure cleaners, was promoting a new handheld electrical window cleaning device, for domestic use. Looking at the product I realised that it had an almost identical head to the robot device I had designed, with twin squeegee blades and the cleaning fluid applied and extracted between them. I don't know whether or not the Karcher engineers got the idea from the now expired robot patent, though it would certainly be legitimate if they did.

A friend commented that that seemed unfair: why should the patent last for only a few years? I disagree. A common misconception is that patents, copyright, and other forms of so-called intellectual property rights reflect some natural right of the inventor/author/composer to a monopoly in the reproduction of their own creative output. This is not the case. A patent was originally seen as a *bargain* between an individual and the state. The state would *grant* a *temporary* monopoly to the inventor, in return for which the inventor must fully disclose how the invention works, such that others may use it, or improve upon it, once the monopoly expires. In other words: it was to benefit society, not just the inventor.

This principle seems to have been forgotten in recent years, in part as a result of intensive lobbying by big corporations – even more so in copyright than in patents – to get the length of the monopoly extended, to the detriment of the benefit to society. I, for one, am opposed to that trend.

I don't know what became of the working prototype robot. The airship hangers remain; the experimental building inside, on which the robot was briefly mounted, has long since gone. It had been built to test the stability of a steel-framed structure under various extreme forms of stress such as floor-loading, wind-shear, and fire. The results were encouraging - even the fiercest fire that they could produce failed to collapse the structure. The data from these experiments have been widely quoted, not least by conspiracy-theorists who believe that the collapse of the twin-towers in September 2001 could not have been caused solely by the collision of the two airplanes. Needless to say, that theory doesn't stand up to more than five minutes' examination. Seventy years earlier, conspiracy theorists would probably have been circulating similar stories about the crash of the R101.

XX

Standing on the shoulders of giants

I 've learned that there's only one important thing in life,' says the philosophical old cowboy played by Jack Palance in *City Slickers*. 'And what's that?' asks the eager young townie played by Billy Crystal. 'That's what you've got to find out!' comes the reply. I know how Crystal's character must have felt: Alan Kay did exactly that to me. Several times.

Alan Kay was already one of my intellectual heroes years before I met him. Sometimes referred to as the father of the personal computer, he and his co-researchers at the Xerox Palo Alto Research Center in the early 1970s came up with many of the core ideas, and the technology to implement them, on which modern computing and indeed much of consumer technology now depend - the graphical user interface, icons and windows, the Ethernet, the laser printer... the list goes on. His detailed vision for the Dynabook, written in 1972, reads like a description of the Apple iPad, launched 38 years later.

Pundits have also noticed the similarities between Dynabook and the eponymous Hitchhikers Guide to the

Galaxy, as conceived by Douglas Adams in the late 1970s. Alan and Douglas subsequently became great friends, and I saw them together on a couple of occasions. Once was at a dinner held within the London Science Museum. I used to have a photograph taken at the museum, sadly since lost, of the two them in standing in front of the replica of Charles Babbage's Difference Engine, one of the earliest sophisticated mechanical computers. They were jointly holding up a hastily-handwritten sign that said 'Don't Panic!' (the opening words from the book).

What sets Alan apart, and perhaps goes some way to explaining the breadth of his inventiveness, is that he is one person who deserves the soubriquet of 'Renaissance Man'. As well as being an eminent computer scientist, one of the few to have been awarded the Turing Medal, he is a microbiologist, historian, and musician - playing many instruments, including the organ that he has installed in the basement of his home. A pipe organ, that is.

His library has more than 5000 books. Each time I met him I would ask him for a new book recommendation. Eventually, he wrote out a comprehensive recommended-reading list, a document that I treasure and have passed on many times. It includes most of the canon of Western thought, some Eastern thinking, history, technology, science, art, design, music...

Alan often speaks in Zen-like riddles, as I alluded to in the opening paragraph. Frustrating at first, the penny eventually drops that he doesn't want to spoon-feed you with his ideas, but encourage you to think out the ideas for yourself. Unlike the hollow epithets of so-called management gurus and life coaches, you find that his riddles reveal more the longer you ponder on them. It took me some years to understand what he meant when he said that you don't really understand something if you only understand it in one way. Or that real intelligence was the ability to hold apparently contradictory ideas in your head *at the same time*.

Alan was also the co-author of SmallTalk, the first fully object-oriented programming language. If object-orientation is the one area of computer science that I claim to understand with some depth, it is in large part due to time spent with Alan. As usual, his answers to my many questions were elliptical, often expressed as challenges through which I would learn the answer. 'Try writing something like HyperCard [a simple but powerful application then available on the Mac] but using only three types of object.' Not a trivial challenge, but when I told him I had managed it he merely said, 'Good. Now try doing it in two,' and then eventually, 'One'. This was to teach me abstraction.

Though he was and is so far above me intellectually, I never felt any condescension. He was a patient teacher, and, indeed, he has spent much time working with young children, exploring new ways to help them learn powerful ideas. What he had no patience for, though, was people who only pretended to understand things. The worst intellectual insult I heard him make about something was, 'It's not even wrong!' meaning that someone's presentation was so vacuous that it contained nothing worth arguing.

Yet what I also saw was tremendous respect for the work of others. If Alan was one of my heroes, it was clear that he had many of his own, both ancient and modern: Thomas Jefferson (pictured opposite - only because I happened to have a drawing of him in my sketchbook), Jean Piaget, Jerome Bruner, Sir Isaac Newton - again the list goes on. Newton is quoted as saying 'If I have seen further, it is only by standing on the shoulders of giants,' and I have heard Alan express the same sentiment many times in different words. He told me that he had dinner once a year with Marvin Minsky, one of the great 20th century thinkers, and Marvin would always greet him with, 'Let me tell you about my new idea, Alan.' 'No, Marvin,' Alan would respond, 'Tell me your old ideas – again – until I understand them.'

XXI

Field of Dreams

'Are you from outta town?' asked the lady at the car rental desk. When we admitted that we were she said, 'In that case I'll send you via the black tops'; we said that would be fine, having no idea what she meant. We were asking for directions from Dubuque to Dyersville; it transpired that 'black tops' meant metaled roads, the locals favouring the shorter route via the 'red tops' (dirt roads). Dyersville, Iowa – population 4000 - was not an obvious destination for a first visit to the United States of America, but that's exactly what I was doing.

My business partner and I were heading for Dyersville to visit Ertl, a toy manufacturer that specialised in die-cast moulding. The cash-cow of the business, if you'll forgive the pun, was agricultural models. Every farmer in the midwest has a John Deere tractor, and every farmer's son has a $1/12^{th}$ scale Ertl model of it. The company's president, Fred Ertl Jr, had no interest in the high-tech toy idea we were, misguidedly, trying to pitch to him, but he was a gracious host and insisted on taking us out to lunch as we had flown so far; though as he drove us into 'downtown' Dyersville he apologised for the limited choice of eateries. We walked into the modest restaurant through the kind of swinging saloon doors that I had previously seen only in Western movies, and the hubbub of conversation died almost immediately, not out of hostility, but merely curiosity at these strangely-accented visitors. Our host recommended the dish of the day from the rather limited menu: barbecue beef and Jell-O. This turned out to be a large plate of beef stew, with potato salad on the side; sitting in the middle of the beef stew was a square slab of strawberry jelly. The idea of mixing sweet and savoury elements on the same plate just doesn't seem wrong to Americans. Perhaps it helps that they just don't have the word 'savoury' in their vocabulary – at least not in the same sense as we English mean it.

Four years after my visit, a farm in Dyersville was selected as the location for filming *Field Of Dreams*. The film stars Kevin Costner as a young farmer who hears a whispering voice amongst the corn rows – 'If you build it, he will come' – and becomes convinced that he must plough up part of his farm to make a baseball pitch. I love the film, but many of my friends profess to loathe it in equal measure. I see powerful narratives of the courage to live out your dreams, of healing, and of reconciliation, and I love the way that your entire understanding of the film changes in the last two minutes. My friends see sentimentality, self-help philosophy, and an absurd obsession with baseball: all the worst aspects of America (in their eyes) rolled into one. The film ends with a distant line of car headlights heading towards the farm, implying fulfilment of the prophecy that the place would become a place of pilgrimage and healing.

The baseball diamond created for the film set is still on that farm in Dyersville, and it has become a real place of pilgrimage, where people seek healing from disappointments, and to affirm dreams. I'd like to go back to Dyersville one day and see it for myself; but I doubt I'll order the barbecue beef and Jell-O again.

XXII

Hospitality

Zaid and Muna were, we gathered, from Jordan. We were at a cocktail party in Harvard: our son, and their grandson, were amongst those graduating. They asked what our son would be doing next, and when we said that Guy had applied to Sandhurst, Zaid mentioned that the present king of Jordan, Abdullah II, and his father, Hussein, had both been through Sandhurst. Making conversation, I offered that I had once come very close to King Hussein, in 1985, at the Ritz-Carlton Hotel in Washington, DC. Waiting for the lift, I was asked by a security man to step aside for a moment; the doors opened and a phalanx of dark-suited men walked out in close-order, several with dark-glasses and semi-concealed ear-pieces; wedged in between them I could just make out the figure of King Hussein, head and shoulders below most of them. '1985, in the Ritz Carlton, Washington?' queried Zaid. Yes. 'I was there,' he said. 'Why was that?' I asked, surprised. 'Well, I was the Prime Minister.'

Zaid Al-Rifa'I, I would later learn, was Prime Minister of Jordon for four governments; his father had been prime minister six times, and his son, Samir, once. You might think that would just about account for the office of prime minister for a lifetime, but the prime minister of Jordan changes quite frequently.

91

The cocktail party was drawing to a close and we said our goodbyes. Zaid and Muna encouraged us to visit their beautiful country one day, and when we said that we hoped to, they invited us to visit them. We understood this to be a politeness not a serious suggestion - we'd met them for just a few minutes only. But Ann and I had talked many times about visiting Petra, and it wasn't many months before we were starting to plan a tour.

That autumn we had a visit from a Jordanian friend of ours, Labib, who lives in Amman but visits the UK regularly. We told him the story of meeting Zaid, and Labib told us that we absolutely must take up the offer: that when an Arab invites you to his home it is meant from the heart and not to be treated as merely a politeness. So when our plans firmed up, I wrote, somewhat tentatively, to Zaid. He replied straight away: we must come to lunch on our first day in Amman.

On the day, he sent his driver, and bodyguard, to collect us from the hotel, in a sleek black extended BMW. Arriving at the walled compound, we entered a pretty, secluded garden, scattered with not a few Roman artefacts. The single-story house was large and elegant, though by no means over-stated. Zaid explained that he'd had it built, along with two further houses for other family members. At the time, friends had chided him for building 'out in the countryside', but today this exclusive residential area is right in the heart of the city. When Zaid's father had moved to Amman shortly after the then Emirate of Transjordan was created in 1921, it had a population of less than 10,000; today it is estimated at 4 million.

We were offered a drink before lunch and Ann asked for a tonic water. I was aware that we were in a Moslem country, and I didn't particularly want an alcoholic drink anyway, but something in Zaid's manner suggested that it was important to him to demonstrate hospitality to a western visitor, so I asked for a whisky, and a very good one it was too, though he did not join me. We then moved to the dining room. The table would easily seat 20, and was laid with enough food for 20, but there were places set for just the four of us. Muna had asked her chef to prepare the most representative dishes of Jordanian cuisine for us to try. We sampled every dish, and each was delicious; when we had eaten our fill, the plates were cleared. It then transpired that we had finished only the first course. Ann and I love fine food, from all over the world, but we are neither of us big eaters.

That day we ate for England.

The conversation was as good as the food: politics, food, politics, history, politics, literature, and so on. I asked Zaid about 'black September' when (in September 1970) King Hussein had militarily attacked the resident groups of Palestinian terrorists that were beginning to threaten the very existence of Jordan, and threw them out of the country. 'Ah, yes, "white September" as I prefer to call it,' said Zaid. Black September became better known as the name of a new terrorist group, equally committed to the overthrow of King Hussein as to the destruction of Israel, and was responsible for the killing of 11 Israeli athletes at the 1972 Munich Olympics.

Not that Zaid's quip was based on a comfortable sense of personal security: I had already read that he was personally the target of an assassination attempt by Black September, escaping with his life but badly wounded when his car was attacked with automatic weapons. That wasn't in Jordan, it was in Kensington High Street - Zaid was the Jordanian ambassador to London at the time. Assassinations are a feature of Middle East politics. The

93

first king of Jordan, Abdullah, was shot dead in 1951 in the Al-Aqsa Mosque in Jerusalem, with his grandson, Hussein, standing by his side. King Hussein, in his turn, was targeted many times, most bizarrely by a member of the household staff substituting sulphuric acid for his nose-drops. On another occasion gunmen opened fire on the king's motorcade, when Zaid was travelling with him. They dived out of the door; Zaid and the king's uncle threw the king into a ditch and dived on top of him to shield his body. All three survived, but Zaid told me, with a wink, that for the rest of his life the king blamed him for his bad back.

Israel was clearly a sensitive subject, though Zaid was quite willing to discuss it. Despite several armed conflicts over the years, Jordan continued to believe that a peaceful settlement of the Arab/Israeli conflict was possible. But the annexation of East Jerusalem and the West Bank was a bitter blow both to the economy, and, perhaps more so, to the pride of Jordan (not that most of the present day Palestinian politicians want to see a return to Jordanian rule). Throughout the '70s and '80s, King Hussein had frequent meetings with Israeli leaders, Zaid present at many of them. All the meetings were held in secret, lest Jordan incur the wrath of its Arab neighbours. Sometimes they were held on a yacht in the middle of the Red Sea, sometimes at the house of the King's personal physician in London, Dr Emmanuel Herbert, a Jew. I sensed Zaid's deep frustration that the Israelis were unwilling to negotiate any compromise.

Having read quite a lot on the subject, it is clear to me that while there were always some 'hawks' in the Israeli leadership who sought to extend the boundaries of Israel, that was not a pre-meditated goal of the six-day war. Yet having gained the West Bank, the national mood clearly changed. When offered very real opportunities to trade land for peace, the Israeli leadership explicitly chose land over peace.

After the lunch we were given a brief tour of the house, finishing in Zaid's study, a wonderfully club-ish room, the shelves filled with antiquities, interesting gifts received in other countries, and photographs of meetings with other world leaders. I asked him who had been his personal favourites; he chose Nixon, rather surprisingly perhaps, 'and Maggie, of course'. We posed for a photograph together, expressed our gratitude for their hospitality, and were driven back to the hotel. We could not believe our good fortune. What an extraordinary and wonderful start, to what would turn out to be one of our most enjoyable holidays together.

Back at the hotel, we were intercepted in the lobby by the hotel manager, saying that he would like to upgrade us to a suite. Whether this was at the prompting of Zaid, I don't know; possibly it was just that the hotel staff had recognised their former prime minister's car and wrongly assumed that we were VIPs.

That evening our friend Labib came to collect us to meet his family for coffee and cake. Labib, having previously lived for some years in East Jerusalem, and travelling back there regularly, has one of only a handful of Israeli-registered cars in Amman. We regaled him with the story of our day. 'I hope you made the most of the suite,' said Labib, grinning, 'If the hotel staff noticed *my* car, they'll probably have downgraded you again by the time you get back!'

XXIII

Underworld

'I think the map room is that way,' said Julian, pointing his flashlight down another dark, dank tunnel. A few yards further and we were there - a long, narrow, but high-ceilinged room with one whole wall covered in a large-scale map of south-east England. 'See if you can find the holes where the drawing pins have been removed,' he urged, bringing the flashlight up close to the map. Most of the holes would mark obvious locations of military, police, and local government buildings, but there would be a few that appeared to be just in the middle of fields or woodlands; they would indicate other possible secret underground facilities, he said.

We were in the Regional Seat of Government at Warren Row near Henley on Thames, one of eleven underground facilities built during the height of the cold war, but now disused. In 1963 a group of activists called Spies for Peace had broken into this one and publicised its existence. Julian implied that he'd also broken into it at one point. I never knew which of Julian's stories to believe, but he did appear to know where to find the map room, and he certainly knew a lot about civil defence, having written a chapter on it for General Sir John Hackett's speculative book *The Third World War*. His brother, Rupert Allason, writing under the name of Nigel West, is an authority on the history of secret services.

The total darkness bar the flashlights gave our own visit a slightly clandestine feel, but it was strictly legal, even if under slightly bogus intent. The Ministry of Defence was selling off the premises and we had feigned interest as potential buyers, simply so we could have a good nose around. The experience was creepy, not just because of the abandoned facilities, but from thinking about all those officials living safely underground while the rest of us would be trying to cope with nuclear fall-out as best we could in the devastation above ground.

Continuing on from the map room we found bunk rooms, kitchens, and massive air filtration units. A very bright hand-held light at the end of another corridor indicated that we were not alone. The other party, we discovered was a television camera crew that had picked up on a visually interesting news story. They asked us why were there. Never one to miss an opportunity for publicity, Julian turned the bull-ometer up to ten. 'Our company designs advanced robots,' he said, 'and we have a big problem with industrial espionage from the Japanese. We need to find a more secure place for our laboratory, with enough room to test the mobile robots.' He'd hooked the fish in one cast. 'Would you be willing to bring some of these robots here and talk about this on camera?' 'I'm a little busy,' said Julian, 'but my colleague, Richard, would be glad to, I'm sure.' In rugby, that's what's known as a hospital pass. They asked me to meet them back there that afternoon, with a working robot, adding the final request that I also bring some technicians 'in white lab coats if possible'.

I returned with one of our autonomous mobile robots, suitably adorned with red flashing lights, and a couple of (human) assistants, attired in white lab coats hastily borrowed from the local school chemistry lab. The interview was conducted by Chris Tarrant, and went out that evening on his prime time *Six O'Clock Show*. It turned out that we were just one of three groups of 'interested buyers' who Chris briefly interviewed for that piece. First came a European couple who wanted somewhere cool to store their wine. 'It's a bit big for a wine cellar, isn't it?' asked Chris. 'We drink a lot of wine,' they said. Next came a bunch of young men dressed in de-mob suits and Nazi uniforms; they had plans for a '1940s themed night club', apparently; it would probably have been popular with Prince Harry, twenty years later. I'm not convinced that either of their stories was any more genuine than our own. Not that the TV crew cared much, I suspect - this was light entertainment, not documentary. I think the bunker was eventually purchased by a document storage company; perhaps the buyers had also been there that day, but that hardly makes for interesting television.

The bunker at Warren Row was No.6 out of a total of 11 such Regional Seats of Government. By the time of our visit, all of them had been officially de-commissioned and their locations no longer classified. Rumours still circulated of a much larger underground *national* seat of government; that rumour was finally confirmed in 2004, when the site was revealed as Burlington in Wiltshire, not far from Bath.

The robot company, which folded in 1989, was the second of the two business ventures that I started with Julian (the first one had been the computer magazine, started while I was still at university in 1979). After that we stayed in contact for years, but latterly our contact had fallen to Christmas cards and the occasional exchange of emails. So I was shocked and deeply saddened to read of his death in The Daily Telegraph in October 2015; he was aged just 67, and had died from complications arising from fairly straightforward heart surgery. The lengthy obituary did bring a smile to my face though. Full of entertaining anecdotes, it might have been written by Julian himself. It certainly captured his lifelong sense of mischief, which I experienced many times first hand, but it also brought out some of his depths. He was a master of self-publicity when he wanted it, but the more serious and worthy side to his nature was conducted away from the public gaze. I miss him.

XXIV

Tradition

'If I were a rich man,' – the words and tune are so familiar that you can't help but sing along. That first line is really a bowdlerization, though. The musical *Fiddler On The Roof*, was inspired by the stories of *Tevye the Dairyman*, written in Yiddish by Solomon Rabinovichunder under his pen name of Sholem Aleichem, the traditional Jewish blessing of 'peace be upon you'. In one of the stories the eponymous Tevye gives a monologue starting '*Ven ikh bin a Rothschild*' – if I were a Rothschild – referring to one of the wealthiest Jewish families in the world, then and now.

It is my favourite musical. I watch the film at least once a year, and have seen several stage versions, including one where Topol played the role of Tevye, as he did in the film. I wonder, were it possible to assess such things, how much of the musical's enduring popularity is due to the catchy musical numbers, and how much to the heart-string-tugging storyline? I love both.

The backdrop to the story is the fate of the Jewish communities in western Russia in the late nineteenth century. In 1881, Tsar Alexander II was assassinated, and, in a pattern that had already recurred many times in history and would recur even more strongly in the twentieth century, the Jews became the scapegoats.

Pogroms were a regular phenomenon, and would lead to an exodus of Jews to Western Europe, the United States, and to Palestine. The musical ends with the whole village of Anatevka carrying their few belongings on their backs, or wheeling handcarts, to seek out a new life elsewhere.

Throughout the story we are party to Tevye's relationship with his creator. He talks to God in a way that is intimate, almost casual - blaming God for his misfortunes, even accusing him of mischief - but always with deep respect. We learn how he regards his religion, along with the traditions of his community, as essential to keeping his balance in the precarious situation.

The core of the plot is the relationship between Tevye and his daughters, as they seek marriage partners. As the story progresses, we witness a progressive break with centuries of tradition. The eldest, Tzeitel, rejects the husband chosen by her father (with help from the semi-official matchmaker, Yente), choosing the poor tailor, Motel, but still seeking her father's blessing. The next daughter, Hodel, announces that she will marry the radical student, Perchik, and does not need her father's blessing. The third, Chava, falls in love with a gentile, and elopes with him. This last break with tradition is too much for Tevye, and he refuses further contact with the couple, treating his beloved 'Chavaleh' (little bird) as dead.

To a modern audience, and especially a gentile, young audience, the attitude of the father must be virtually incomprehensible - it is *obviously* he who is in the wrong, not just with his attitude to Chava, but to all three of them. As so often, I find myself with very mixed feelings about it, and for me that is part of the power of the story. Because leaving aside the specific rights or wrongs of these stories, once you take the view that neither community tradition nor religious belief should ever be allowed to trump personal freedoms, it is very hard to see what role there is for either in a modern society. I find that disturbing.

Not that Tevye's deep love for his children is ever in doubt. There are certain scenes that are guaranteed to get me going: when he and Golda pray a blessing on their daughters at the start of the Sabbath meal ('May the Lord protect and defend you'); at Tzeitel's wedding ('Is this the little girl I carried?'); and when he and Hodel say goodbye at the station not knowing if they will see each other again.

The last time I saw Fiddler on the Roof performed on stage, Tevye was played by Paul Michael Glaser (pictured overleaf – in that role). He is best known to my generation as one half of the television detective duo *Starsky and Hutch*, but a few years before that, Glaser had played the role of Perchik, the radical young student, in the 1974 film version of Fiddler. I saw a billboard advertisement for this new stage production in Dublin and went to see it on my own during a business trip. Paul Michael Glaser was outstanding: he *owned* the role; he was animated, yet completely relaxed; his performance included some noticeable homage to Topol, but at the same time he brought his own unique style to it. As soon as I left the theatre in Dublin I booked again for the last available performance of the tour, in London. I went with Ann and we took a couple of friends; I wish now that I had thrown caution to the wind and taken everyone I know.

Quite apart from his performance as Tevye, there was something special about Glaser's graduation from playing the role of Perchik, more than forty years previously. At seventy years of age, it was an appropriate progression for him as an actor. But to me it was more than that: it reflects the pattern that we see in real life. Isn't it true that most of us gradually morph from playing the role of Perchik, the

young radical wanting to change the world, to that of Tevye, fighting a rear-guard action against the erosion of our most precious traditions.

XXV

Thanksgiving

Americajin. That's the only word I can make out from what the old lady has been saying to me - American. 'Watashi-wa Igirisujin,' I manage to respond - I am English - but this doesn't put her off. 'Something, something, something, Americajin, something,' she says again. 'Wakarimasen,' I stammer, repeatedly: I don't understand. And with that I've pretty much exhausted my knowledge of Japanese.

I am standing in the basement of a department store in the Ginza, the upmarket shopping district in Tokyo. The basement is a food hall, not unlike that of Harrods in London, but with wonderfully different produce. I am whiling away time between business meetings, enjoying the unfamiliarity of the city. The strangest thing about Japan, someone had told me before I went, is that almost all the stories you've heard about it turn out to be true: they really do line up on the platform opposite where the door will be when the train stops; there really are wax models of the dishes in the restaurant windows; they really do reshuffle the seating order in a business meeting every time someone new comes in. Japan is a strange place to Western eyes; not strange as in hostile, but strange as in different and surprising.

The old woman talking excitedly to me is, I assume, just another shopper; she isn't wearing a uniform like a member of staff. She's maybe 70 years old, and quite wizened. Undeterred by my protestations she continues to talk to me in Japanese, and by this stage has her hand on my arm; it's starting to feel just a little awkward. Then she reaches into her shopping bag and pulls out a small packet of biscuits wrapped in cellophane and ribbon, and thrusts them into my hand. More talking. Reaching into her bag again she next withdraws some banknotes. I interpret this to mean that I she wants some money for the biscuits, though I can't imagine why she would think I would want them. But no, she takes the crisp new bank notes - about fifty US dollars' worth - and places them in my other hand. Then after some further rapid sentences, of which I understand not one word, she turns around and walks off.

I look around for the hidden camera, my first guess being that I am going to appear on one of those weird Japanese television shows. But I can see no camera, and no-one approaches me, even when I eventually leave the store. The next day I tell the story to several of the Japanese businessmen I meet with. I watch their faces for knowing smiles, as in, 'Ah yes, I see you fell for the old-lady-with-the-biscuits trick.' No, they seem as perplexed as I, unable to offer an explanation.

Eventually, one man tells me that, though he isn't sure, he thinks it might be that the old lady was repaying a kindness done to her by an American, possibly many years ago. Given her age (this occurred in 1986), it might even date back to the post-war MacArthur administration. That many Japanese have such a positive view of the USA is in large part due to the way that they were treated during this period; the occupying Americans sought neither revenge nor compensation, but simply to rebuild the nation, though on more democratic lines. Perhaps this lady had received a personal kindness from an American soldier, and had been unable to repay it previously. Perhaps she had just come into some money or made a small winning on the state lottery – the notes were crisp and new after all – and went looking for the first Western man she could find, assuming him to be American. This is pure speculation, but it's more plausible than any other explanation I can come up with.

I never saw the old lady again. I, cautiously at first, ate the biscuits, which were delicate and delicious, and treated myself to a nice dinner with the money. But the episode left a lasting impression, causing me to think about the nature of giving thanks. Over the years since, I have learned two things, several times over. The first is that the most powerful way to express thanks for a kindness is to pass on a kindness to someone else. Secondly, that saying thank you to the giver many years after the event can sometimes be more powerful than saying thank you straight away.

'You should send a copy to Dr Brown.' My first book, *The Robot Book*, had just been published, signalling the start of my brief career as a robot designer, and I'd just given a copy to my parents. Now my mother was urging me to send a copy to a man I barely knew: our family doctor for just a few years, whom I hadn't seen since I was nine years old, and had no idea how to contact. 'Surely, you remember? Whenever he came to the house [doctors did house calls in those days] and saw you playing with your Meccano, he would encourage you to be an inventor when you grew up. I'm sure he'd be interested to see the book.' Privately I doubted he'd be interested in the book, and would certainly have no memory of me, but I didn't argue.

It took quite an effort to get an address for Dr Brown, who had long since retired: the NHS isn't keen on giving out private addresses for doctors, even retired ones, but there are some advantages to having spent a few years in journalism. I sent a signed copy of the book, with a letter explaining the context, letting him know that I now was an inventor, and thanking him for taking an interest and encouraging me all those years ago.

Two days later a handwritten letter came back; I still have it, and I still well-up whenever I re-read it. It begins, 'Dear Richard, This is one of the most exciting days of my life,' continuing for four pages. He said he did just remember me – the fact that we lived in the manse probably helped – but had no memory of the conversation about becoming an inventor. He was evidently deeply touched that I had written to him, going on to say, with misplaced modesty, 'I shall treasure [your letter] as evidence that my 32 years in general practice was not entirely unprofitable to my patients.'

It made me realise how much a simple word of thanks can mean to someone, especially many years down the line. I have several times since then written a letter to someone who did a kindness to me many years ago and for which, in many cases, I had never said thank you at the time. I have had several moving responses back.

The Robot Book was not a bestseller, though, surprisingly to me, it was translated into both Spanish and Serbo-Croat. By the end of the 1980s it was out of print in all languages. Many years later, I received an email from a lady named Marisa, proprietor of a small bookshop in Madrid, asking if I was the Richard Pawson (the name isn't quite as unusual as I once imagined) who wrote *El Libro Del Robot* If so, did I know where she might obtain a copy, as she had a request from a customer? I confirmed that I was the author, but that I had no idea where she might obtain a copy. I added that the field of robotics had advanced a long way in recent years and my book was now out of date, so her client would be well-advised to look for a more recent one.

She thanked me, adding that the customer knew that there were more up-to-date books, but was looking specifically for my book. I looked across at the bookshelves in my study and noted that I still had the two free author's copies of the Spanish edition. I certainly had no need for two; even one was a vanity since I couldn't read a word of Spanish. So I sent Marisa the book with my compliments, and I was delighted to receive in return a present of some Spanish sausage from her home region, with instructions on how to eat it: on lightly toasted bread spread with olive oil and crushed tomatoes. Delicious.

I wrote back once more, asking, just out of curiosity, why the customer wanted the book. She replied on his behalf, expressing his regret that he had no English with which to reply directly. Her customer, Javier, had borrowed my book several times from his local library when he was a boy, and built some of the working model robots for which the book contained plans. Javier was now a qualified computer engineer, specializing in robotics. He had wanted to find his own copy of the book that had had 'such an influence on his life and career'.

That one story made the whole effort of writing that book worthwhile. I realised then what Dr Brown had felt. What we value most is not the 'thank-you': it is simply the knowledge that we made a difference to someone's life.

Index

2001 a Space Odyssey, 63
Abdullah, King, 91
Africa, 69
airship, 81
Aldrin, Buzz, 2
Aleichem, Sholem, 101
Alexander II, Tsar, 101
Alexander, Chris, 33, 59
Allason, Julian, 97
Al-Rifa'I, Zaid, 91
Amman, 92
Annapurna, 13
Apollo, 1, 40, 57
Armageddon, 10
Armstrong, Neil, 2
Artificial Intelligence, 64
Artificial Life, 64
Arup, Ove, 60
Auschwitz, 17
Australia, 60, 74
Babbage, Charles, 86
Bale, Christian, 68
Balfour, Earl of, 46
Balfour, Lady Alison, 47
Bath, 53, 99
BBC, 56
Begin, Menachem, 12
Beit She'an, 9
Beit She'an, Israel, 9
Bergen Belsen, 46
Berlin, Isaiah, 12
Black September, 93
Blade Runner, 63

Boston, 2, 49
Bruner, Jerome, 87
BRE, 81
Burke, James, 55
Byron, Lord, 63
Cardington, 81
Centre Point, 83
Chapel Hill, NC, 21
Charles, Prince, 34
Chicago, 49
Churchill, Winston, 75
Clarkson, Jeremy, 39
Commodore, 1, 17
Concorde, 39
Cope, Lady Djemila, 53
Costner, Kevin, 90
Cradle Runways Ltd, 82
Crystal, Billy, 85
Der Spiegel, 45
Disney Institute, 7
Domingo, Placido, 53
Dublin, 103
Dubuque, IA, 89
Duke University, 22
Dyersville, IA, 89
Dynabook, 85
Edinburgh University, 46
Edwards, Betty, 5
English Channel, 76
Ertl, Fred Jr, 89
Ethernet, 85
Feng Shui, 33
Feyerabend, Paul, 56

Field Of Dreams, 90
Frankenstein, 63
Gere, Richard, 59
Gill, AA, 56
Glaser, Paul Michael, 103
Guernsey, 76
Hackett, Gen. Sir John, 97
Hannover, 17
Harry, HRH Prince, 99
Harvard University, 37
Hasbro, Inc, 66
Henley on Thames, 39, 97
Herb Simon, 45
Herbert, Emmanuel, 94
Herod the Great, 11
Himalayas, 78
Hussein, King, 91
HyperCard, 87
intellectual property, 84
Ireland, 29
Irwin, James, 1
Israel, 9, 46, 94
Japan, 46, 66, 77, 107
Jefferson, Thomas, 87
Jerusalem, 9, 51, 94, 95
John Deere, 89
Jordan, 91
Kastner, Rudolf, 46
Kathmandu, 13, 15
Kay, Alan, 7, 85
Kremer, Tom, 66
Kuhn, Thomas, 56
Liberia, 25, 26
Lindenmayer, Aristid, 36
Lodz, 17
Londolozi reserve, 70
Lord of the Rings, 81
Los Angeles, 46
Lunar Module, 1
MacArthur, Douglas, 108

Machpuchare, 14
Madanat, Labib, 92
Magic Circle, 30
McCarthy, John, 64
Meccano, 109
Megiddo, 10
Mengele, Joseph, 17
Mercury (space), 22
Michelmore, Cliff, 57
Minsky, Marvin, 37, 88
MIT, 36
Monrovia, 25
Montefiore, Sir Moses, 10
Naked Objects, 78
Negroponte, Nicholas, 36
Nepal, 13
New York, 40
Newcastle University, 82
Ngala game reserve, 71
OCS Group, 82
Palance, Jack, 85
Palestine, 47, 94, 102
Palladio, Andrea, 35
Palm Springs, 56
Pappert, Seymour, 87
patent, 82
Pavarotti, Luicano, 53
Pawson, John, 77
Piaget, Jean, 87
Plato, 33
Pokhara, 13, 79
Popper, Carl, 56
Princeton University, 22
Prometheus, 63
Rabinovichunder,
    Solomon, 101
Robotics, 82, 109
Rothschild, Baron, 47, 101
Rubik, Erno, 43
Saint-Exupéry, Antoine 78

San Diego, 35
Scamp, 64
Science Museum, 86
Scott, Doug, 78
Serbo-Croat, 110
Shelley, Mary, 63
Sherpas, 14
SmallTalk, 87
South Africa, 70
Spafford, family, 49
Sperry, Roger, 6
Starsky and Hutch, 103
Suleiman, 9
Sydney Opera House, 59
Syria, 51
Tarrant, Chris, 99
The Matrix, 75
The Three Tenors, 53
Tokyo, 46, 107

Topol, 101
Tramiel, Jack, 17
Vanguard Conferences, 35
Turing Medal, 86
North Carolina Univ., 21
USA, 66
Utzon, Jørn, 60
Vitruvius, 35, 60
Warren Row, 97
Washington, DC, 91
window cleaning, 82
Wittgenstein, Ludwig, 56
Wogan, Terry, 67
Xerox Parc, 85
Yeager, Chuck, 22
Yeoh, Francis, 52
Yorkshire, 77
Zen, 77, 86
Zionism, 46

Printed in Great Britain
by Amazon

81407570R00072